how2become

Special Air Service
The Insider's Guide

Orders: Please contact How2become Ltd, Suite 2, 50 Churchill Square Business Centre, Kings Hill, Kent ME19 4YU.

Telephone: (44) 0845 643 1299 - Lines are open Monday to Friday 9am until 5pm. Fax: (44) 01732 525965. You can also order via the e mail address info@how2become.co.uk.

ISBN: 978-1-907558-06-1

First published 2010

Typeset for How2become Ltd by Good Golly Design, Canada, goodgolly.ca

Printed in Great Britain for How2become Ltd by: CMP (uk) Limited, Poole, Dorset.

CONTENTS

WELCOME

Welcome to your new guide, how to join the Special Air Service: The Insider's Guide. As you are probably already aware, the SAS are a unique breed of people who are both professional and extremely skilled in everything they do. They have deservedly earned the reputation for being *the* most professional and respected force in the world, bar none. This book is not designed to give you the 'Hollywood' perspective of joining the SAS; instead it will give you simple facts about what the selection process involves, and how to pass it.

The Special Air Service (SAS) is the British Army's most renowned Special Forces unit. From the moment several black-clad figures appeared on the balconies of the Iranian Embassy in London in 1980, interest in the SAS intensified. Their motto, 'Who Dares Wins', has become part of British popular culture. The selection process for joining the SAS is extremely tough. It is not about brute strength or having the ability to kill without fear; but instead it is about extreme mental focus, an in-depth desire to join, and an unbelievable level of physical fitness.

The purpose of this guide is to give you an insight into the selection process and to also assist those members of the Armed Forces who are considering, or even attending, UK Special Forces selection.

Best wishes,

The how2become team

The How2become team

PREFACE

By Author Richard McMunn

The majority of soldiers who put themselves up for Special Forces selection will fail. This is simply due to the fact that their *desire* to join is based on either their 'ego', or the perceived celebrity status that most of us would believe goes with joining such an elite force. That perceived celebrity status is something that I personally have a lot to be thankful for; because without it, nobody would buy this book. An uncomfortable fact maybe, but it is the truth. Since the Iranian Embassy siege in the 1980's, the status of, and the interest in the SAS has taken a sharp incline. It also made the SAS the most feared fighting unit in the world, which for the top tier of the British Army, is an invaluable asset. However, with perceived fame and glory, there comes a price. Increased interest in the SAS has meant a greater emphasis on security, not only to protect the men who join it, but more importantly the secret intelligence that protects the British people.

The vast majority of missions that the SAS have been in, or are involved in, are never made public knowledge, and

there is a very good reason for this. One of the most potent weapons in the arsenal of the Special Air Service is secrecy. Without secrecy they cannot perform the tasks that they do. The majority of missions they undertake are deep behind enemy lines and this type of work takes a very special person, and an equally special mindset. All of us have our own idea of what your average SAS soldier looks like. To the majority of us, he will be 6 feet tall, built like a brick shit house, and generally look like someone who there's no way in a million years you'd pick a fight with. Whilst there are a few people of this calibre in the Regiment, the majority of them are people whom you wouldn't give a second glance to if they walked past you in the street. That in itself is a very powerful weapon.

During this guide I will cut out the hype and crap that surrounds the SAS. I will give you the basic facts that you need to know in order to pass selection. I understand that the majority of people who read this book will have no intention of ever going through SAS selection. However, for the small percentage of people who are putting themselves through the process, you will find this book an invaluable resource in your preparation.

So, I expect you want to know something about me? Well, to begin with I have never been in the SAS, nor have I been through selection. So what qualifies me to write a book on how to join the SAS? During my time I have known two people who have come into contact with the SAS. The first person is someone who failed selection, and the second person is someone who passed it. I worked with both of them in the Fire Service during the early 1990's and up until 2009, and I still keep in regular contact with them today. Surprisingly enough, the person who failed selection gave me a far greater insight into what a candidate goes through. I was extremely

surprised that he'd failed, simply because he was a lot fitter than the person who had passed selection. However, after spending time with both of them, and discussing the selection process in depth, it soon became apparent that my initial perceived thoughts of what SAS selection entailed were entirely rubbish. Just like the majority of people out there, I had this vision that pure physical strength and fitness were the most important elements of selection. Whilst these are important, there are other areas that a candidate must concentrate on in the build up to selection. It is these areas that I will focus on during the content of this guide.

So, what does it take to become an SAS soldier? As I'm sure you already know you must be a serving member of the Armed Forces in order to apply. The majority of candidates who put themselves forward are either from the Parachute Regiment, the Royal Marines, the RAF Regiment and the Royal Engineers. The selection processes for these careers themselves are tough enough; but they are nothing compared to SAS selection. Nobody who goes through selection finds it easy. It takes a special kind of person to pass it. However, even if a person does get to the end of the selection process, there are no guarantees that he will be accepted. If the recruitment team does not like them for any reason, then they simply won't get selected.

DESIRE FIRST, FITNESS SECOND

I mentioned at the beginning of my preface the word *desire*. Desire is crucial if a soldier is going to have any chance of passing selection. For desire breads confidence, desire breads intense preparation, and desire breads focus. If you want something *really* badly, then you can have it. Anybody who puts themselves up for selection must have an in-depth

CHAPTER I

INTRODUCTION

Shrouded in secrecy, the Special Air Service is the world's finest of all Special Forces. Founded by David Stirling, the SAS were the first counterterrorism unit to be invented, and whilst many other Special Forces have copied their tactics, they still remain the unequivocal leaders in their field. This does not mean to say that other Special Forces are incompetent or of no worth, in fact the exact opposite. However, the SAS are, and always will be, the finest Special Operations Unit in the world.

As the war on terror intensifies, so does the professionalism and determination required of the SAS. Always attempting to stay one step ahead of their enemies, the SAS are blind without the use of dependant and reliable intelligence. More recent events only prove the need for such an elite fighting force and the SAS motto 'Who Dares Wins' is indicative of their attitude and determination to conquer terrorism. The SAS counterterrorist role was first introduced following the massacre of Israeli athletes in Munich, 1972, during the Olympic Games. The purpose of the Games was to

celebrate peace and, for the first ten days, everything went well. However, in the early hours of the 5th of September, eight Palestinian terrorists succeeded in breaking into the Olympic Village, where they killed two members of the Israeli team and took nine more hostages. In an ensuing battle, all nine Israeli hostages were killed including five of the terrorists and one on-duty police officer.

In 1980 the SAS were first witnessed on global television, when they stormed the Iranian Embassy after a large number of people were taken hostage. This was the first time that the general public, and in fact the international community, had witnessed such a fearsome fighting force. For the Government, the vision of the Special Air Service abseiling down the Embassy prior to their insertion was seen as a useful deterrent to any 'would be' terrorist or terrorist group. There were of course downsides to this incident. Interest in the SAS fiercely intensified overnight and the need to protect both the men that served in the Regiment, and what it stood for, needed to be protected at all costs.

During the Falklands War in 1982 the SAS were able to demonstrate more of their traditional fighting skills by patrolling the Islands and looting out vital targets. The SAS had landed in the Falkland Islands well before the main fighting force had arrived. This enabled them to feedback vital information to the Commanding Officers who were responsible for the operation. The problem with the Falkland Islands is that it is under cloud for much of the time. This meant that any satellite or overhead reconnaissance mission was unable to pick up a clear indication of what exactly was happening on the ground. The SAS provided this information by careful and planned observations of the islands well before the troops arrived. They were inserted by Sea King helicopters deep into the night before trekking for miles to

their target location, without any support or protection other than their own weapons. On Pebble Island the Argentinean Force had placed a number of fighter aircraft, based ready for action, on a small landing strip.

The SAS positioned themselves in tiny bunkers overlooking the strip for days on end. They gradually placed demolition charges and explosives on the aircraft in locations that would go undetected by the enemy. Once the battle began, the Royal Air Force and Royal Navy Fleet Air Arm attacked the base and the SAS detonated the charges. This was the first the Argentinean Force knew that they were being attacked. This demonstration of skill and bravery by the Special Air Service only reiterates their professionalism. The level of training they receive is astounding, and their fitness, determination and commitment is nothing less than highly commendable.

THE SAS BERET

The SAS beret is beige in colour and the famous 'winged dagger' badge sits in the middle. The badge, which is found on the beret itself, is comprised of the following three elements:

- The sword, which represents Excalibur (the legendary sword of King Arthur).

- Two upswept pale blue feathered wings, which are supported by red centres.

- At the lower end of the blade is a black scrolled ribbon, which bears the SAS motto 'Who dares wins'. This is in the same colour as the feathered wings.

All of the above are located on a black cloth background, which is attached to the beige beret.

The SAS badge

The parachute wings

The parachute or 'sabre' wings are worn on the right shoulder by members of the SAS. The wings were said to have been designed by Lieutenant Lewes in around 1941.

The idea for the wings came after he allegedly saw a fresco of an ibis, a large bird with a long curved bill, in an Egyptian hotel.

SAS RANK STRUCTURE

The Special Air Service rank structure is the same as for the regular British Army, as follows:

TROOPER

▼

LANCE CORPORAL

▼

CORPORAL

▼

SERGEANT

▼

STAFF SERGEANT

WEAPONS USED BY THE SAS

The type of weapons used by the SAS regiment will very much depend on the assignment or mission they are undertaking. For example, the SAS would not use an H&K MP5 in long-range combat or an AK-47 for the same scenario. Like in sports, the elite exercising sportsman will know the strength and weakness of the tool he is using, and so do the SAS. The following is a list of some of the more common weapons used by the regiment in recent years.

Heckler & Koch Modern Assault Rifle

The G3 is a very reliable weapon under almost all conditions – small, compact and perfect for close combat. This weapon was used by the SAS in Northern Ireland.

Type	Automatic
Range	400 meters
Calibre	7.62 mm
Weight	4.4 kilos
Velocity	5 - 600 rpm
Magazine	20 rounds

Kalashnikov AK47

This is not the most precise weapon, but the SAS are aware of its weaknesses.

Type	Automatic
Range	300 meters
Calibre	7.62 mm
Weight	4.3 kilos
Velocity	600 rpm
Magazine	30 rounds

M16

The Colt M16 is produced in almost the same number as the AK47, but in many different versions. Because of the 5.56 mm ammunition, it is possible for each soldier to carry more rounds. It was supposed to be a self-cleaning weapon, but it was not. It was used by the SAS in Borneo 1963-66, Aden 1964-67, Oman 1970-76 and the Falkland Islands 1982.

Type	Automatic
Range	400 meters
Calibre	5.56
Weight	3.4 kilos
Velocity	7 - 900 rpm
Magazine	20 to 30 rounds

SA80

The SA80 is not a great weapon, although it is the predominant weapon used by the British Army. There is a tendency for the

magazine to fall off and the shaft can break. The SA80 is used by the SAS on some occasions, but they are acutely aware of the weapon's weaknesses.

Type	Semi-automatic
Range	300 meters
Calibre	5.56
Weight	3.8 kilos
Velocity	650 - 800 rpm
Magazine	30 rounds

SIG Sauer P226

This pistol measures 7.7 inches overall and weighs approximately 29 ounces. It is one of the most compact of the high-capacity 9mm automatics, being similar in size to the Colt Commander, albeit a little wider.

The P226 has one of the most compact, comfortable handles of any 9mm featuring a double-column magazine. The frame has no rear strap, and the black plastic grips are of the wrap-around type. The front strap is serrated, and the front of the trigger guard is squared and serrated for those who favour a "finger forward" two-hand hold.

THE SAS AT WORK

More often than not the SAS will operate in four man teams, and there is a very good reason for this. Four has been determined as the number that is sufficient enough to carry all of the equipment and resources in order to get the job done, and it is also a sufficiently small enough number for them to go largely undetected. Remember that the SAS will usually operate deep behind enemy lines and there will sometimes be a requirement for them to split up if their presence is detected by enemy forces. This is one of the reasons why the SAS assesses a candidate for their ability to 'operate independently' during the selection process. The candidate's ability to work as part of team will have already been assessed during their initial recruit selection, and let's be honest, if a Royal Marines Commando or Paratrooper isn't capable of working competently in a team environment, then he shouldn't be in there in the first place. Working as a four man team also allows the SAS to safely escape from a combat situation with an injured member of their team. Let's assume that one of the four man team gets injured during a fire fight. A four man team will allow two soldiers to carry the injured person out, whilst the fourth man covers their egress. If the team were to be a three man team, then this scenario would immediately fail as there would be nobody to provide cover.

Patrolling

Once a solider has successfully passed selection, he will then embark on an intensive period of training. The vast majority of people who join the Regiment will come from an infantry unit such as the Parachute Regiment, therefore their soldiering and patrolling skills will already be at a competent level. However, what they won't be competent in is the ability

to operate and patrol as part of a four man team. This training will form part of the Jungle Training phase which is explained further during a later section of this guide.

During training an SAS soldier will be highly trained in the following key areas:

movement

camouflage

setting ambushes

anti-ambush drills

contact drills

emergency rendezvous skills

During SAS movements the four man team will usually progress in single file. Each member of the team will have a specific 'area' to protect. They must focus on this area intently and rely upon the remainder of the team to protect each of their designated areas too. The last man in the file will normally carry a belt fed machine gun, simply because he will have a far greater area to cover than the rest of the team. Each member of the four man team will specialise in a specific area. Take a look at the following:

SAS Medic

Each four man team will have a solider that is highly trained as a medic. This is for obvious reasons. If a soldier is designated to be a medic then he will undergo a series of training modules, both at Hereford and also at a real-life hospital. Because of the nature of work that the SAS undertake, i.e. deep behind enemy lines, there is strong chance that a member of the team could become injured. Without the presence of a medic they are seriously compromised. The medic can also provide medical assistance to civilians in a combat area which can

lead to the winning over of informants and other influential people within a combat zone or area. This is more commonly known as 'hearts and minds'.

SAS signaller

A signaller is probably *the* most important member of the four man patrol. Without communications the team are going nowhere and they won't be able to successfully complete their mission, or provide HQ with vital information relating to intelligence and reconnaissance. They also rely on the signaller to provide them with vital information from base HQ, and it also provides HQ with their whereabouts if they need to retract quickly from a zone or area. The signaller will be competent in Morse code and the remainder of the four man team with also have basic knowledge on how to operate the equipment. Out of all of the members of the four man SAS team, the signaller is target number one for enemy sources. Without communications, the four man team are severely penalised.

SAS Linguist

Language skills are vital to the four man SAS team. Even more so when they are dealing with members of local native communities, and also when liaising with foreign troops. Whilst not as important as the Signaller, the Linguist is still a key factor in the make up of the formidable SAS four man patrol team. SAS soldiers are taught languages at the Army School of Languages in Beaconsfield and usually followed up by a visit to the respective country to practice using their skills in real life situations.

SAS Forward Air Controllers (FAC)

The SAS Forward Air Controller will only form part of the four man team if the mission or situation requires it. Unlike the Signaller and Medic, the FAC is only required during extreme

situations that require the complex skill of directing aircraft in to attack enemy ground targets. In order to be a competent FAC the SAS soldier will need to be extremely proficient in map reading, and also have the ability to convey complex information to the pilot whilst under extreme pressurised situations. In most cases, he will only get one chance to get it right.

SAS Demolition expert

No SAS four man patrol team would be complete without the addition of a demolitions expert. Following training, a complex and comprehensive demolition training course is undertaken by those chosen to specialise in this field. Part of the course involves learning how to choose the right explosives for the job, where to place the charge, and also which targets to use for greatest effect.

During the next chapter we will take a brief look into the history of the SAS and some of the more famous situations they have been involved in during recent years.

CHAPTER 2
THE HISTORY OF THE SAS

The Special Air Service was originally founded by Lieutenant David Stirling during World War II. The initial purpose of the regiment was to be a long-range desert patrol group required to conduct raids and sabotage operations far behind enemy lines. Lieutenant Stirling was a member of Number 8 Commando and he specifically looked for recruits who were both talented and individual specialists in their field, and who also had initiative.

The first mission of the SAS turned out to be a disaster. They were operating in support of Field Marshal Claude Auchinleck's attack in November 1941, but only 22 out of 62 SAS troopers deployed reached the rendezvous point. However, Stirling still managed to organise another attack against the German airfields at Aqedabia, Site and Agheila, which successfully destroyed 61 enemy aircraft without a single casualty. After that, the 1st SAS earned regimental status and Stirling's brother Bill begun to arrange a second regiment called Number 2 SAS. It was during the desert war that they performed a number of successful insertion

missions and destroyed many aircraft and fuel depots in the process. Their success contributed towards Hitler issuing his Kommandobefehl order to execute all captured Commandos.

The Germans then stepped up security and as a result the SAS changed their tactics. They used jeeps armed with Vickers K machine guns and used tracer ammunition to ignite fuel and aircraft. When the Italians captured David Stirling, he ended up in Colditz castle as a prisoner of war for the remainder of the war. His brother, Bill Stirling, and 'Paddy' Blair Mayne, then took command of the regiment. Prior to the Normandy Invasion, SAS men were inserted into France as 4-men teams to help maquisards of the French Resistance. In Operation Houndsmith, 144 SAS men parachuted with jeeps and supplies into Dijon, France. During and after D-Day they continued their raids against fuel depots, communications centres and railways. They did suffer casualties however and at one stage the Germans executed 24 SAS soldiers and a US Air Force pilot. At the end of the war, the SAS hunted down SS and Gestapo officers. By the end of the war the SAS had been expanded to five regiments, including two French and one Belgian.

By the 1960s, the SAS had almost no overseas commitments at all due to the fact that Britain had given up almost all of its colonies. During this period, however, there were numerous political battles and rebellions taking shape in the form of communist sponsored guerrillas who besieged many of these newly formed countries. The guerrillas often resorted to different tactics such as assassination, rape and kidnap. Some of these countries were protected by the British, and the Special Air Service once again found itself involved in these wars. Lieutenant Colonel John Waddy was the Commanding Officer of the SAS at this time and

he suggested that the SAS attempted to combat terrorism in three different ways. The first method was by means of collecting intelligence on terrorist groups, something that the SAS are still used for today. He also recommended that they respond to specific terrorist incidents (such as the Iranian Embassy hostage taking) and finally pre-empt terrorist actions. The latter is probably the hardest task for the SAS in today's terrorist climate. The September the 11th bombings only go to prove that with all the intelligence in the world it is very difficult to stop a terrorist who is hell-bent on destruction and war. As a result of these recommendations, the Counter-Revolutionary Warfare Wing (CRW) was set up in order to provide security for the rulers and officials of these protected countries. The SAS members of the CRW would protect the VIPs and also collect intelligence on any active terrorist groups known to be operating in the area. Even today, the Counter-Revolutionary Warfare Wing of the SAS still provides Close Personal Protection for VIPs.

Today, the SAS are more active than ever in their pursuit to protect the country from the ever-increasing threat of terrorist activity.

SAS BATTLE HONOURS

Second World War:

- North Africa, 1941-43

- Tobruk, 1941

- Benghazi Raid, 1942

- Landing in Sicily, 1943

- Termoli, Valli di Comacchio, Italy, 1943-45

- Greece, 1944-45

- Adriatic, Middle East, 1943-44

- Normandy and North-West Europe 1944-45

Falkland Islands, 1982

Western Iraq, 1991

Western Iraq, 2003

THE SIEGE OF THE IRANIAN EMBASSY

On the 20th of April 1980 the SAS were called into action following the siege of the Iranian Embassy in London. That morning the SAS teams were practising their normal drills at the 'Killing House' in Hereford (the SAS base), which involved groups of 4 soldiers making their way through the house searching for suspects and firing off live ammunition. This drill was something that they were all familiar with, and it was very well rehearsed.

At approximately 1145 hours a call was received at Hereford informing the Commanding Officer that the Iranian Embassy in London had been taken hostage. Immediately the soldiers set about preparing themselves for the mission and the resulting journey down to London. Most of them made their way down to London in unmarked cars and they arrived at Regent's Park Barracks early that evening, where they prepared themselves for the mission.

The facts of the terrorist siege were now becoming clearer. Six men, who had arrived in Britain the week before, had managed to force their way into the Iranian Embassy, pulled out their weapons and claimed to be from an organisation that was fighting for the Independence of Arabistan. In total

they took 26 people hostage. Of those 26 people, one was a policeman, two were sound engineers from the BBC and the remainder were Iranian members of staff. The body that is normally responsible for authorising SAS missions is known as the JOC (Joint Operations Centre). The current Director of the SAS at that particular time, Brigadier de la Billiere, sat on the JOC, but because the incident was a terrorist incident with political implications, the go ahead needed to be given by COBRA (Cabinet Office Briefing Room), which reports directly to the Prime Minister, who was Margaret Thatcher at that particular time.

As the incident progressed the leader of the terrorist group, who was called Oan, demanded that an aircraft take them and their hostages to an unnamed country. At this time the Police were in control of the incident and were negotiating with the terrorists. Over a period of time the terrorists agreed to release 5 hostages in return for food, water and an agreement for Oan's demands to be televised on national television.

The SAS began to prepare for the mission by constructing a small wooden model of the Embassy. Luckily, one of the hostages who had been released was one of the BBC sound engineers and he was able to give the SAS some vital information about the layout of the building. In addition to him, the caretaker for the building was also able to give valuable information about the building's layout and structure. One of the major problems faced by the SAS was the fact that the windows were bullet proof and therefore would need to be blasted with explosive charges in order to break entry.

Eventually, the SAS assault team moved out of Regent's Park Barracks, made their way to a side street near to the Embassy, and then waited for the go ahead to storm the

building. The wait for the assault team was long and tiresome but this was what they were trained for. On the evening of the 2nd of May the assault team carried out a reconnaissance mission across the rooftops leading up to the Embassy. It was during this mission that they noticed that an entry could be made through a skylight window. However, it wasn't until the 5th of May that the SAS actually stormed the Embassy and this was as a result of shots being heard from inside the Embassy.

The threat by Oan, the leader of the terrorists, to kill his hostages had been carried out and the body of the hostage he had murdered was thrown out of the front of the building at approximately 19:00 hours that evening. The Police immediately decided that it was time for the SAS to storm the building and at 19:07 hours the commanding officer of the Police handed a signed written request to the commander of the SAS, Mike Rose, requesting that the SAS raid the building.

Negotiations continued with the terrorists where false arrangements were made for a coach to pick up them and their hostages and take them to the airport. In the meantime the SAS assault team was moving into number 14, which was the Royal College of Physicians, located directly next door to the Embassy. At 19:23 hours the SAS stormed the building. They created a diversion at the front of the building in the form of demolition charges and CS gas. The remainder of the team accessed the building from the rear and also by abseiling down from the roof and into the building through the first floor windows. The leader of the SAS team (soldier 'I') made his way through the front of the building where SAS soldiers broke down the door with their sledgehammers.

As the SAS made their way through the building, searching and securing the floors, they noticed Oan standing on the

landing of the first floor with a gun in his hand. As he was about to shoot, the Policeman who was being held as a hostage, managed to wrestle him to the ground. An SAS soldier told him to move out of the way before he shot Oan down to the ground with his Heckler and Koch. The SAS knew that as soon as they stormed the building, the terrorists would begin to panic in the ensuing mayhem. As a result the terrorists began to shoot wildly, killing a hostage and injuring a number of others in the process. As the SAS made their way up to the second floor where the hostages were being held, the terrorists threw down their weapons and tried to mingle in with the hostages in an attempt to escape capture. The SAS team asked the hostages quickly to identify the terrorists and a number of them were taken out right there in the room.

The assault team then made their way out of the building to the rear and began to tie up the hostages, just in case any of them were unidentified terrorists. As they did so a terrorist with a grenade in his hand made his way down the rear stairs to the back lawn. An SAS soldier noticed the terrorist and was about to shoot him when he noticed two of his colleagues standing at the bottom of the stairs in his direct line of fire. Instead, he hit the terrorist hard on the back of his head with his rifle before his colleagues shot him, ensuring that he was dead. The mission took just over 10 minutes to complete and once over, the SAS team was hurried away in vans to a secret briefing at Regent's Park Barracks, where Margaret and Dennis Thatcher congratulated them before they finally returned to Hereford. The fact that the whole SAS raid was filmed on television was thought of as a positive thing by the British Government. They felt that the successful raid would act as a deterrent to other potential terrorists who were considering attacking Britain. Once the siege

was over and the dust had settled, revelations began to appear stating that the SAS killed hostages even after they had surrendered.

Although this information will never be truly confirmed, it is thought that the SAS were told to kill all terrorists and leave nobody alive, even if they surrendered. The thinking behind this is that any terrorist prisoners held in the UK would only encourage other terrorists to carry out such acts in revenge or in an attempt to have their counterparts released.

THE GIBRALTAR SHOOTINGS

The Gibraltar shootings are another well-documented case of SAS activity. One of the main reasons for it being so well documented is the fact that the SAS soldiers who carried out the killings ended up in the European Courts standing trial for unlawful killing. The whole saga came about following the identification of IRA members Sean Savage and Daniel McCan in Spain during 1987. Following their discovery, the MI5 set up an intelligence gathering operation in an attempt to determine why they were present in Gibraltar. Intelligence gathered suggested that the terrorists intended to target the resident military band, which played at the changing of the guard outside the Governor's residency. Further intelligence suggested that the IRA had perfected a 'push button' remote controlled bomb, which could be triggered in the pocket of any coat jacket.

Another member of the IRA, Mairhead Farrell, was also seen in Gibraltar at that time, further fuelling the concern and speculation amongst the British Government that an attack was imminent. The Spanish Police were briefed and asked to follow the trio when they arrived at Malaga airport on the 4th of March 1988. Unfortunately, the Spanish Police lost trace of

the three, which meant a search of the area had to be made in order to relocate them. A further IRA member had also been seen in the area where the military band performed, once again providing speculation that an attack was due any day. As a result, a 16-strong SAS team, including an explosives expert, was flown out to Gibraltar. It was anticipated that the IRA would use a car bomb detonated by a remote control push button. On the 6th of March the SAS strategically placed themselves around the area in small groups of two or three. Their task was to look out for the three IRA members, who were believed to be armed and in possession of the remote control devices that would trigger the bomb.

At some point, IRA member Savage was seen loitering in the area of a white Renault 5 located in the square where the changing of the guard usually took place. He was seen to open the door of the car and fiddle around with something inside, which was believed to be a device that made the bomb live, ready for the changing of the guard. One of the SAS members went out to the vicinity of the Renault 5 to see if he could see any signs of any explosives. The only thing that he noticed was that the relatively new car had a rusty aerial, which indicated to him that the car had been tampered with in some way, and therefore could contain an explosive device.

Following this period all three IRA members were seen walking out of Gibraltar towards the Spanish border. They were then followed by four SAS soldiers, who were dressed in casual clothing consisting of jeans and lightweight jackets, each armed with Browning pistols. As they followed the IRA members they noticed that Savage then began to walk in another direction, back towards the town. This forced the SAS team to split up into two groups of two. One group stayed with McCan and Farrell whilst the other two followed

Savage. At about the same time a Police siren was heard in the area and this seemed to unrest the IRA members to the point that one of them looked around and made eye contact with one of the SAS soldiers. The SAS soldier reached for his pistol and was about to issue a challenge when he noticed McCan put his arm across his jacket. The soldier believed McCan was about to reach for a button that would trigger the explosive so he shot him in the back. At the same point Farrell appeared to reach for her bag so the same soldier shot her too.

At this point the second SAS soldier also shot both McCan and Farrell. During this sequence of events Savage, who was on his way back to town, had turned around to see what was happening. He appeared to reach for his pocket and at this point both SAS soldiers who were tasked with following him, shot him dead.

CHAPTER 3
THE SAS STATE OF MIND

Adopting the right state of mind is crucial if a solider is to have any chance of passing SAS selection. In simple terms, mindset is the habitual or characteristic mental attitude that determines how you will interpret and respond to certain situations. Let's assume that you are on selection. You are taking part in phase one of SAS selection and you are tabbing on the Brecon Beacons. You are required to tab 12 miles in thick rain and fog, your feet are hurting from the blisters that are forming on both feet, you are hungry and tired, and your mind is telling you to give in. What do you do? It's at this point that you have to focus your mind on exactly what it is you want to achieve, and this effectively comes down to one factor – desire. How much do you want this? How much are you prepared to go and how hard are you willing to push yourself? I can safely say that one of the most important elements of your ability to pass selection is your desire. Forget your physical capabilities for a second, how much do you want it? In order to get through every stage of selection a soldier must have an in-depth sense of desire to join the SAS. Without desire, he will not pass.

Cast your mind back to the preface when I explained about how surprised I was that the person who failed SAS selection was the fittest of the two. When I asked him why he thought he had failed selection, he simply said 'because it was way too tough and I just couldn't go any further'. Although the person who passed selection was not as fit, his *desire* to pass ran far deeper.

DESIRE

Let me give you an example of how desire can make a huge difference in what you want to achieve. During my career I have been in many types of situation where either my life depended on my will to survive, or my desire to achieve would see me through to a successful outcome. One situation in particular was whilst serving as a firefighter on White Watch at Maidstone Fire Station. It was approximately 17:45 hours on a cold winter's afternoon and I was due to go off shift at 18:00 hours. It was a Friday and I was looking forward to going out on the town with my mates. All of a sudden, the bells went down and we were turned out to a fire in a furniture store located in the town centre. When we arrived, thick black smoke was billowing out of the front entrance door and windows, and a rather stressful shop owner was standing there urging us to get a move on. As you can imagine, his shop was in serious danger of burning to the ground, and his entire business and livelihood that had taken him years to build would go down with it. I'd not long been out of my recruit training and I had not experienced that many 'severe' fires yet. Although I was just about to find out first hand what a severe fire was and how it could hurt you. It was my turn to wear breathing apparatus so I quickly got rigged up, went under air, and then followed the more senior firefighter into the building. What was about

to happen was one of the most frightening experiences I have ever encountered in my life. I was about to be tested to the limit.

As we entered the building I could sense something wasn't quite right. You know when things are not quite right – it's your intuition. The smoke was becoming thicker and blacker by the second and the temperature was rising quickly. The signs of flashover and backdraught were relatively new to the Fire Service at the time, so we weren't fully aware of the dangerous situation we were entering into. We made our way up to the third floor quickly, taking a hose with us so that we could tackle the fire, and more importantly retrace our steps on the way out. We had been told that the fire was probably in a room on the upper floors of the building, so we started to search for the fire in line with our training and procedures.

After approximately ten minutes the heat inside the building became unbearable, and I couldn't see my hand in front of my face due to the thick, black acrid smoke. I concentrated on my training, took deep breaths and checked my air regularly. I was very fit at the time and hadn't used that much air from my cylinder. My colleague shouted in my ear that he couldn't see the fire anywhere and that maybe we should start thinking about evacuating the building due to the intensity of the heat. I think his words were something more along the lines of *"let's get the fuck out of here, the heat's starting to burn my shoulders!"*

Just as we started to retrace our steps we heard a noise that was every firefighter's worst nightmare. Outside, the fire had become so intense that the officer in charge had decided it was time to get us out. Basically, he had initiated the evacuation procedure, which was short blasts of an acme thunderer whistle. All we could hear from inside the building

was whistles being blown – we knew we were in trouble. Even though it was a long time ago now, the thought of it still makes the hairs stand up on the back of my neck. I'd heard of incidents where firefighters had lost their lives in fires, and I thought that it might now be my turn.

We quickly started to retrace our steps, following the hose carefully. I'd started to become slightly disorientated due to the heat, but I knew the hose reel would guide us back down the stairs, and to ultimate safety. How wrong could I be! As we approached the top of the stairs the hose suddenly disappeared. My colleague turned to me and shouted that the hose had become trapped under some fallen furniture and he couldn't find the other end of it – we were now in serious trouble. The hose was basically our lifeline, which would lead us to safety, and now we didn't have it. We sat together and took deep breaths. The whistles were still blaring outside and we knew that the only way to get out of this damn building was to try as hard as possible to conserve our air and remain calm. All I could think about was my girlfriend and how much I wanted to see her again. If you've ever been in a situation where you feel like your life is going to end at any second, then you'll know how frightening and distressing it is.

We decided to locate a wall, and then simply follow it in the direction that our instincts told us would lead to the top of the stairs. We eventually came to the top of some stairs but there was a problem. We could not locate the hose, which effectively meant that this flight of stairs was not the flight we had used to gain access to the building in the first place. Basically we had no choice, we had to go down them and just hope that they led us outside. As we progressed down the stairs my heart was beating like never before. I remember thinking that these stairs could be leading us to a cellar or

basement area and that we would become trapped – it was a gamble that we had to take. Thankfully, as we made our way down the stairs we heard voices. The officer in charge had sent in an emergency crew to help locate us. We met them halfway down the stairs and they then led us out to safety. I can remember making my way outside of the building and looking back at the store, which had already been half demolished by the inferno. Another few minutes in there and I would have been dead, that's for sure. As I took off my breathing apparatus set, which was caked in soot, the officer in charge looked over at me with a huge sign of relief on his face. If only he knew how I was feeling!

I learnt a tremendous amount from that incident. The first thing I learnt was how important it is to remain calm in every crisis situation. Even when things are *really* bad, the only way that you'll achieve a successful outcome is by staying calm and focusing your mind on what you want to achieve. The second thing I learnt from that experience was the importance of comradeship and teamwork. The Fire Service is very similar to the SAS in the fact that everyone looks out for each other. Everyone in the team is dependant on each other. You do your job properly and the team will be just fine. Break the rules, be unprofessional or disorganised, and things will go wrong, it's as simple as that!

Desire and a will to succeed is just one of the many attributes a soldier will need in order to pass selection. Let's take a look at a few more.

CONFIDENCE

Confidence is at the top of the list for me personally when it comes to achieving what I want in life. There is a vast difference, however, between confidence and arrogance. I

am confident because I believe in my own abilities, I work hard to improve on my weak areas, and I also believe in those people around me. I am not afraid to take risks that I believe are worth taking, and I am certainly not afraid to put my own life at risk to save others.

Whilst going through SAS selection try to demonstrate confidence, but never cross the line into arrogance. The selection staff want to see that you have the guts to keep running when you're absolutely shattered, and when your body is telling you stop. They want to see that that you have the confidence to put yourself forward, when others around you stand back. Confidence comes with time and with experience, but there is no reason why you can't start improving it right now in preparation for selection.

STRENGTH

To the majority of people, the word 'strength' means the ability to lift heavy weights or objects. To the SAS soldier, it is not just about *physical* strength, but also about strength of the *mind*. The only obstacle in your way to passing selection is your own mind. Fill it with doubt and negative thoughts, and the end result is virtually guaranteed to be failure. Yes, of course you must work on your physical strength and fitness, but if your mind isn't tuned into what you want to achieve, then you are going nowhere.

Allow me to give you an example of where strength of mind can work to your advantage. Whilst going through the selection process for becoming a firefighter, I was required to attend an intense physical assessment day. Amongst other things, the assessment involved a requirement to:

Bench press 50kg, 20 times within 60 seconds;

Run around a field for an hour whilst carrying a heavy object between a small group;

A claustrophobia test involving crawling through sewer pipes in the dark whilst wearing a blacked out mask;

Assembling items of equipment;

Knots and lines;

Hose running.

The hose running assessment was carried out at the end of the day. Out of twenty people who had started the day, there were just six of us left. Although I was exhausted, there was absolutely no way I was going to fail the hose running assessment. This assessment had a reputation for being gruelling. It entailed running out lengths of heavy hose whilst wearing full firefighting uniform, and then making it back up again in a prescribed manner. It sounds like a simple task, but coupled with the sheer exhaustion that was already taking its toll on my body, and the fact that I was wearing an ill-fitting firefighter's uniform, this was no easy task.

The Station Officer started off by making us do ten runs, just to warm up. Whilst we were carrying out the runs, a Sub Officer would walk next to us shouting in our ears how 'useless' he thought we were, and that he knew 'how much we wanted to give in'. He also made a couple of remarks about my mother which I won't go into! After the first ten runs we were then required to do a further 25 more in succession. Soon after we started, two men dropped out, leaving just the four of us remaining. The four of us managed to complete the 25 runs, although I was ready crumble and I know for certain that I couldn't have done any more. We all stood there in a line with our hoses made up, ready for the next set of instructions. The Station Officer walked up and down with

his stick and clipboard, making us wait in anticipation – he clearly loved every minute of it. My legs were shaking and I could feel my heart pounding so fast it felt like it was about to jump out of my skin. Then, the Station Officer spoke once more – "OK, pick up your hoses and get ready for another 25 runs". 25 more runs I thought! You must be joking!

At that point I was at a crossroads in my life. Give in now and all that hard work training to pass firefighter selection would be out of the window. But if I try to press on, then there's absolutely no way I can manage another 25 runs. It was at that point that a thought came into my mind. Whether I could do the next set of 25 runs or not was irrelevant. What was important was that I carried on and I didn't give in. So I did. I picked up my hose and waited for the Station Officer to tell us to commence. He then turned round and said – "Well done guys, you've passed. Put the hoses down and grab yourselves a glass of water." I couldn't believe it; the bastard was just testing us to see if we had the strength of mind to continue, even though our bodies couldn't take anymore – a valuable lesson in determination and strength of mind if ever I saw one.

Mindset is extremely important whilst preparing for SAS selection. You will need to be organised and disciplined and you will need to concentrate on improving your weak areas. Mindset is not just important whilst out tabbing on heavy terrain, it is also important during stage 3 of the selection process, which is Escape & Evasion and Tactical Questioning. You will spend hours with a black bag over your head, naked, whilst standing in an extremely uncomfortable position. Let's assume you've been standing in the same position with a black bag over your head, freezing cold, starving and dehydrated for 18 hours. Eventually they come and get you and sit you down for an hour's worth of

interrogation and questioning. You say nothing, except your name, rank, number and date of birth. They keep grilling you constantly, trying to get you to crack. Then, after an hours worth of interrogation, they tell you that you're going to now do 24 hours against the wall, naked and with the black bag over your head again. What do you do now? You decide.

BEING INDEPENDENT

The quality of independence is all about being able to look after yourself and being capable of carrying out your role within the team to a professional standard. The majority of soldiers who put themselves up for selection should be highly competent at being independent. However, being independent in the Royal Marines, the REME, RAF Regiment or the Parachute Regiment is very different to being independent in the SAS. Just about every selection process for the Armed Forces involves some form of team assessment. Not the SAS. They will assess your ability to work on your own, simply because that's what you will have to do on occasions during missions deep behind enemy lines.

Now of course, there are many other qualities required in order to become a soldier with the SAS. You have to be very good at map reading, and you certainly need to specialise in a certain area. Top level soldiering is also crucial. If you're an average soldier, then you simply won't get accepted.

I can remember talking to a Regimental Sergeant major in the Royal Marines who told me about a time when he had worked with the SAS in Afghanistan. He told me how these guys were phenomenal at what they did. *"They were all shit hot at everything they did!"* were his exact words. That just about sums the SAS up.

PREPARING FOR SAS SELECTION

Before we move on to the selection process and how you can pass it, I want to give you a number of crucial tips that will assist you. They are simple tips, but choose to neglect them and you will fail.

TIP I

The right mental approach

Without the correct mental approach your chances of passing selection will be limited. Let me pose a question. What do you think your average SAS soldier looks like? A 6 feet tall, 16 stone muscle bound thug? This couldn't be further from the truth. Whilst there are these types of people in the SAS, the majority of people who join are medium-sized, average-looking men. The majority of them would easily fit into a crowd and go unnoticed. That is the reason why the SAS don't go all out to take on men who just fit the bill of 'body-builder'. Don't think 16 stone, think more like 12 stone, and you'll be getting closer to the type of person who joins the SAS.

So, what has all this got to do with mental approach? The point I am making here is that you don't need to spend hours in the gym lifting weights in order to get ready for selection. With regards to fitness training, I recommend a series of intense basic exercises such as running, walking with weight, swimming and light weight workouts. The right mental approach includes not only your desire to pass selection, but also your mental approach to the type of pre-selection training that you carry out. You will also need to eat the right types of food (carbohydrate high), and drink plenty of water. Finally, and I will cover these later, you must be competent with a compass, be capable of reading a map, and be able to effectively deal with blisters.

 how2become

TIP 2

Use an action plan to ensure success

Action plans are a great way to measure your progress during pre-selection preparation. I use an action plan in just about everything I do that is work related. An action plan basically sets out what you intend to do, and when you intend to do it. An example of a very basic action plan that is focused on fitness preparation might look like this:

Monday 6am start
run 6 miles (best effort), and record my time.

Tuesday 6 am start
50 press-ups, 50 sit-ups, making sure I concentrate on the correct technique. Swim one mile of my local pool (64 lengths).

Wednesday
10-mile run, then 50 sit-ups and 50 press-ups, making sure I concentrate on the correct technique.

Thursday
30 mile cycle ride and then 4 mile run.

Friday 6am start
10 pull-ups, 50 press-ups and 50 sit-ups, making sure I concentrate on the correct technique.

Saturday Rest day.

Sunday
15 mile brisk walk carrying 25kg Bergen.

During the next week you may decide to increase the intensity of your workouts, alternate the rest days and increase the number of repetitions that you are performing.

If you use an action plan, then you are far more likely to

make significant progress. If you stick the action plan in a prominent position in your living quarters, then it will act as a reminder of what you need to do the following day.

TIP 3

Train hard and selection will be slightly easier

If somebody finds a test or assessment easy, it generally means that they have prepared hard for it. If you work hard in the months leading up to selection, then you will find parts of it easier than if you did little or no training whatsoever. The SAS only recruit twice a year, and the selection process takes place regardless of the weather. Even if it's freezing cold and snowing, selection still goes ahead. The first stages of selection are easier than the latter. The trouble is, once you get to the latter stages your mental and physical fitness levels will be suffering, regardless of how fit you are. If you have done little or no physical training, then you are simply not going to pass the latter stages.

When I was 26 I decided to carry out an Iron Man challenge for a local charity. This involved swimming 2 miles, then running a marathon, before finishing off with a 120-mile cycle ride. I managed to achieve all of this within 9 hours. Whilst it was mentally tough, the physical aspect was relatively easy. It was easy because I'd trained extremely hard in the 6 months leading up to the challenge. Train hard in the build up to SAS selection and you will find certain elements easier. It is important to have plenty of reserve for the final stages of selection.

TIP 4

You are what you eat (and drink)

Let's face it; a diet of lager, burgers, chips and kebabs isn't going to help you get the most out of your training sessions.

In the build up to selection fill yourself with the right types of foods and also make sure you drink plenty of water. You will need the water to keep yourself hydrated.

Foods such as fish, chicken, vegetables, fruit, rice and potatoes are all rich in the right types of nutrients, which will allow you to perform to the best of your ability. Try to cut out caffeine, alcohol and all forms of takeaway food in the build up to selection. You will feel a lot better for it and you will be able to work harder and longer.

TIP 5

Map reading competence

Whilst I will dedicate a further section of the guide to navigating your way around the terrain used during selection, this is a very important tip that should not be neglected. It is crucial that your map reading competence is exceptional. If you take a slightly wrong turn during selection, then this can have severe consequences. Not only can it cost you precious time, it can also lead to failure. If you can't read a map and compass, then you shouldn't be up for selection.

TIP 6

Be good with blisters

Being good with blisters is not just learning how to deal with them when they do occur, but also being able to take appropriate steps to limit their chances of occurring in the first place. During a later section of this guide I will cover blisters in-depth, and more importantly how to deal with them. Remember that a small thing such as blister can totally screw up your chances of passing. Literally scores of people leave selection due to blisters. Don't be one of them.

Let's now move on to recruitment and selection for the SAS.

CHAPTER 4
RECRUITMENT AND SELECTION

During this section of the guide I will cover the selection process and what each part entails. It is important to indicate from the outset that, whilst I will make reference to the Brecon Beacons during this section, the SAS do use alternative locations, such as the Scottish Highlands. The reason for the change in venue is simple. Over time, and as interest from the general public and media intensified, the location of SAS selection had become known to many people. There had been a number of occasions where the general public, whilst innocently strolling through the Brecon Beacons, became confronted by a soldier running like mad with an SA80 rifle and Bergen on his back. There had been too many complaints from members of the public, and that ultimately led to the British Army choosing alternative locations.

The selection process for entry into the SAS is undoubtedly the toughest of any of the worldwide Special Forces. The selection process now comes under the umbrella of UK

Special Forces selection; simply because it also includes those who wish to join the Special Boat Service. The selection process is now the same for both the SAS and the SBS. What makes the selection process so tough is the fact that it tests both one's physical and mental stamina over a prolonged period of time. Many other selection processes for different armed forces units are shorter, and less rigorous. The reason for the intense difficulty of the process is because it is imperative that the SAS get the right men for the job. There is no room for error during any of their missions and it requires a special type of person to be able to hold down that level of responsibility.

The SAS tend to recruit from the Parachute Regiment and the Royal Marines, although members do include soldiers from other regiments of the British Forces including the Royal Engineers, the Royal Artillery and the RAF Regiment. The SAS soldier is both physically and mentally tough. They are certainly not robots or supermen, but instead extremely fit, highly skilled and totally focused on the task at hand. You will never see an SAS soldier bragging in the pubs about the fact that he belongs to the Regiment, nor will you see him fighting with anyone in the streets when the pubs close. They are highly professional and very guarded about the role that they play. The average SAS member is not 6ft tall with a weight of 16 stone, but is more likely to be around 5ft 8 inches and of a build, appearance and stature of somebody who would quite easily blend into a crowd of people and go unnoticed. Underneath this disguised exterior, however, is an immensely fit and skilled soldier. Ask any SAS soldier and all of them will tell you that they found the selection process difficult. Not one of them will ever say it was easy, because it simply isn't!

THE SPECIAL FORCES BRIEFING COURSE (SFBC)

Selection starts back at a soldier's own regiment, where he must request through his NCO that he would like to be put forward for selection. The initial phase of selection is for the soldier to attend a Special Forces Briefing Course (SFBC).

The SFBC runs twice a year, usually over a weekend period. The course is designed to give those candidates who wish to go through selection the chance to taste what life in the SAS is all about. It also gives the SAS the chance to see if they like you. The weekend SFBC course usually starts on a Friday evening when candidates arrive at the SAS base, Sterling Lines, in Hereford. During the SFBC you will be given a number of briefings and presentations that are designed to show you what the SAS is all about. It will also give you an indication as to what to expect during the tough selection process. On the first evening of the course you will undergo a series of tests that include map reading, map memory test, first aid test, general military knowledge test and an IQ test. The type of physical tests that you will undertake during the SFBC will not be too difficult although a number of people do surprisingly fail them. Before you undertake the SFBC make sure you can reach at least level 14 on the Bleep Test, you can swim 100 metres fully clothed in under 3 minutes, and that you can tread water for 15 minutes. You will also be required to pass the standard Army Basic Fitness Test (BFT), which shouldn't be a problem for any soldier who is on the course. In addition to the BFT you will also be required to pass a Combat Fitness Test, which involves a 2-mile run in 18 minutes and an 8-mile run in 1 hour 40 minutes. Make sure you can pass these with ease.

Whether you are invited back to Hereford to take part in the full SAS selection process will be up to the SAS themselves.

If they have any doubt about your potential then you won't be going back.

THE RECRUITMENT STAFF

It is certainly worth writing a few lines about the recruitment staff who assess candidates that put themselves up for selection. The stereotypical view of them is not surprising. Most people believe they are total nutters, who are out to make you fail at all costs. This couldn't be further from the truth. SAS selection staff are in fact current serving SAS soldiers. It makes sense for them to select the people who they will eventually serve alongside. This is quite a refreshing change to the usual type of selection process that forms part of many organisations and public sector bodies today. For example, before I left the Fire Service, a large majority of Brigades had started to farm out their recruitment of firefighters to third party organisations. As you can imagine, these external organisations had no idea about what it took to become a firefighter. It was their job to simply tick boxes and look for keywords and phrases in a persons application form. This to me was madness. Surely the right people to assess potential firefighters for joining the job were those people who already served in the job? Thankfully, the Armed Forces still retains a lot of the common sense principles that have made them so good at what they do. Therefore, the SAS themselves will select candidates, and nobody else.

If you met a serving member of the SAS you would probably be surprised at both what they look like, and also how they act. They are generally well humoured (you'd have to be to do their job), chilled out and non-confrontational. Of course, you wouldn't want to mess with them, but overall they are decent people who quietly go about their business. If you

were to ever get on the wrong side of them, then you'll know about it. Earlier in the guide I spoke about the lad whom I served with as a firefighter. He was of the same ilk; very laid back, very good at his job but you would certainly never mess with him. He was a martial arts instructor in his spare time, something which he had learnt during his time in the forces. Because of their nature, the serving SAS soldiers who act as recruitment staff are not out to make the candidate's job any harder than it has to be. After all, they themselves have been through selection, but more importantly they will have to serve with you if you make it through selection. The last thing they want is to have to work with you during a real life mission when they have made your life purgatory during selection. The selection process does its own job of whittling out those who are unsuitable, without any of the staff having to physically hurt or bully anyone. As I'm sure you'll agree bullies are aresholes who are not fit to walk the earth that we live on. Bullying during a selection process doesn't serve to select the right people. It just makes the bully's ego grow and makes them feel good that they have control over the person they are intimidating. The SAS don't need to do that. If somebody fails selection, then it will be because they either pull out themselves, or their face doesn't fit.

IF YOUR FACE DOESN'T FIT, YOU'RE NOT GETTING IN!

The truth is, if you successfully manage to complete the selection process, you won't be accepted unless your face fits. It's not one of those jobs where a candidate is protected by 'fairness and equality'. If they don't like you then you simply aren't joining them. This happens quite a lot during selection. A candidate will do everything he can to pass and nothing can break him, only to find out that he will not be

joining the Regiment. It is something that a candidate must be prepared for before he puts himself up for selection.

Anyone who goes through the process must come recommended by their SNCO. There will be plenty of vetting checks before they accept you and if you have a history of being incompetent or there are disciplinary problems in your home regiment or troop, then again you won't be joining. The key to passing selection is to arrive there with a good background and a strong recommendation from your SNCO. It also helps if you specialise in a specific area, or if you are shit hot at some part of your job. Picture the scene, a soldier from the Royal Electrical and Mechanical Engineers (REME) works as a Vehicle Mechanic. Not only is he one of the best Vehicle Mechanics in his Regiment, but he is also a highly respected 'all round' competent soldier. This gives him an advantage over your average Vehicle Mechanic who is never going to set the world alight. If both of them are up for SAS selection, which one of the two is more likely to be wanted by the SAS?

THE SAS SELECTION PROCESS

Selection takes place twice a year, either in the heat of the summer or in the cold of the winter. Candidates who are up for selection are usually exemplary soldiers with an unblemished service record to date, a high level of physical and mental fitness and, more often than not, specialists in their field.

The SAS is full of soldiers who are exceptional at different things. After all, that's what makes a team like the SAS work so well, the fact that its members are not single-minded people. They all bring something special to the unit and are purely focused on getting the job done. The tasks and

missions they are presented with are more often than not out of the realms of 'normal soldiering'. Any up and coming star soldier who asks his NCO to be put forward for SAS selection is likely to meet slight resistance. After all, why would an NCO want to lose such a promising young soldier to 'The Regiment'? Any soldiers who put themselves forward must first of all be fully aware of the high failure rate. The figure is around the 95% mark and those who fail selection are returned to unit (RTU'd) immediately. They are permitted to try again for selection one more time after a 6-month period has elapsed. The selection process for the SAS is not the same as the regular Army. Whilst the process of selection for the Parachute Regiment and the Royal Marines is extremely tough, it is nowhere near as difficult as the selection process for the Special Air Service.

When candidates arrive for selection at the SAS base in Hereford you would expect them to be greeted with shouts and instructions from a fierce SAS NCO, but this is not the case. Candidates are expected, in the majority, to look after themselves and be at a certain place at a certain time. If they are late or put one foot wrong, then they are back on the first train home. The well-prepared candidate for selection will have been training for months in advance, and I mean months!

It is virtually impossible to pass the SAS selection process without intensive and dedicated preparation, yet still some soldiers arrive for selection having carried out little or no preparation. Serving SAS soldiers must be able to fend for themselves and they must have the ability to think for themselves. Nobody will be there to tell you to get up in the morning and nobody will tell you to get your arse down the gym in order to get fit.

The level of fitness required in order to successfully pass the SAS selection process is exceptional. Having the ability to reach level 16 on the bleep test or being able to bench press 100kg is not the aim of the game. You won't find any muscle bound tossers in the SAS, in fact the exact opposite. Their fitness is predominantly based on the ability to keep going under extreme conditions and for prolonged periods. This requires a different level of fitness than that of the athlete who can run a marathon in under 3.5 hours or the swimmer who swims the channel in record time. It's about prolonged physical and mental fitness such as trekking 50 miles across rough terrain in freezing conditions with a 16kg Bergen on your back before carrying out a difficult surveillance mission in a small hole for days at a time without being spotted.

The average day during selection will commence at around 4am. Most days you'll be required to get up and out of bed yourself. It is totally up to you to get up and make sure you are mustered at the rendezvous point on time and with all of your equipment. If you're not there, then the truck will leave without you and you'll be returned to unit that same day. You cannot afford to make any mistakes during the selection process, which makes it all the more difficult to succeed, especially when you hardly get any sleep either. Those who fail are usually glad to go back to unit.

Once on the truck, you will be dropped off at various different points and it is up to you to make your way back to a specific point within a certain time using a prismatic compass, your map, and the map reading skills you have gained over the years as a regular soldier. This stage of the process usually takes place in the Brecon Beacons or the Black Hills of South Wales. However, in 2006 the Special Forces selection team were forced to take this stage up

into the Scottish Highlands. The Brecon Beacons National Park is open to the public and there had been too many occasions when camera mad tourists had been snapping candidates going through their paces during selection. In addition to this problem, the site of a soldier on selection running towards you carrying a rifle had frightened too many members of the public. So, even though reference is made to the Brecon Beacons throughout the duration of this guide, there is a possibility that the Scottish Highlands will be used as an alternative safer location.

During this phase of the process you will have to carry a heavy Bergen, a weapon, and sometimes ammunition boxes over a series of long timed hikes, navigating between different checkpoints. Positioned at each checkpoint will be a serving SAS soldier who will not offer any words of encouragement or criticism. These are known as Directing Staff (DS). Once you eventually reach the rendezvous point, which is usually late into the evening, you may then be told that there has been a mistake and the rendezvous point has now changed and is a further 15-mile trek away. As you can imagine, at this point many people drop out or resign. It is only those people who keep going without moaning who get to realise that the truck is actually just round the corner or a mile down the road. It is imperative that the SAS get the people they want during selection and there is no time for moaning or whining. A job needs to be done and every member of the regiment must be able to operate both individually and as part of a team. If one person lets the team down then the whole mission will fail. The demands of life in a Special Forces unit such as the SAS require each member to be self-motivated and self-reliant; therefore it is imperative that each person can fend for himself.

PHASE 1 – ENDURANCE WEEK 1

Battle fitness test (BFT)

The first 3 weeks of SAS selection are known as the 'endurance' phase. The main aim of the endurance phase is to test a soldier's physical fitness and mental stamina and it is at this stage of the process where most people drop out.

During a soldier's initial recruitment training he is often provided with encouragement and the mere fact that he is being shouted at to get a move on will drive him forward. The SAS selection process is somewhat different and there is nobody there to shout orders or in fact any words of encouragement. This makes it a very lonely place and the SAS believe that if you want to be a part of their regiment then you will not need any encouragement to pass their tough selection process. In order to pass this stage of the selection process a soldier will need to be highly determined and have the ability to look after himself. The first part of the selection test requires candidates to pass the standard Army Battle Fitness test (BFT). Surprisingly, this test will lose between 5 and 10% of the candidate group who are returned to unit immediately. If a candidate who puts himself up for selection cannot pass the standard Army Battle Fitness Test then understandably he will not proceed any further. The BFT consists of a 3-mile run – the first half must be completed within twelve and a half minutes and for the remainder there is no time limit. The BFT is carried out whilst carrying a 40lb Bergen and a rifle. The remainder of week 1 is comprised of map revision, orienteering lessons, plenty of gym work, beastings, 5-mile runs, 8-mile runs and the Fan Dance.

Map reading revision

During the first week you will be provided with a basic map reading course. Make sure you take notice during the

lesson and listen carefully to what you are being told. As you progress through this guide you will realise that your ability to read a map quickly and accurately is essential. See Insider tip number 4 for more information and tips in relation to map reading and also a later chapter of the guide 'how to use a compass'.

Swimming assessment

During the first week you will need to pass a basic swimming test which is performed at a local swimming pool. You will be required to swim around the outside of the pool whilst wearing combat clothing and trainers. Once you have completed the circuit you are then required to tread water for 15 minutes. Once this stage has been successfully completed you are required to swim a length underwater.

Orienteering

During selection you will be required to take part in a number of orienteering exercises. Orienteering derives from the Swedish word "orienteering" and the term was first used to describe the sport in 1918 by Major Ernst Killander who was then the President of the Stockholm Amateur Athletic Association. Orienteering originated in Scandinavia and was used as a military exercise during the late 19th century.

Orienteering is basically a running sport that involves navigation with a map and a compass. The traditional form involves cross-country running, although other forms have evolved such as 'ski-orienteering'. During selection you will be required to pass a number of orienteering exercises, which normally take place in the Forest of Dean. Each exercise is timed and you will complete them with at least one further soldier who is also on selection. You will be required to carry a 40lb Bergen during the orienteering exercises, which can be difficult if your orienteering skills are not up to scratch.

The aim of the orienteering exercises is to navigate round all of the points on the provided map in the correct order, and in the fastest possible time. You will be encouraged to improve your time at each checkpoint. In order to obtain a good time during the orienteering exercises you will need to be a fast runner (if you are up for selection then you should be anyway), with strength and stamina. You will also need good concentration levels in order to navigate your way through the terrain.

At each checkpoint along the course there will be the SAS Directing Staff (DS) to check that you have passed through that particular point. The DS at each checkpoint will record the time you checked in at so that at the end of the exercise, all your times can be added together to determine whether or not you completed the course in sufficient time.

Physical exercise sessions

Physical Exercise sessions, or 'beastings' as they are more commonly known, are a common part of Army life and whilst they are frowned upon in the public eye, they are an important way to assess a soldier's ability to withstand constant and relentless physical and mental pressure. During selection you will succumb to a number of highly physical exercise sessions that can last up to 2 hours and involve many different exercises. During these sessions you will carry out hundreds of press ups, sit ups, star jumps, shuttle runs, sprints, running up steep hills. You name it, you'll be doing it!

The FAN Dance

During the first week comes the 'Fan Dance'. The 'Fan Dance' is where each of the remaining soldiers has to climb and then descend the dreaded 3,000ft Pen-y-Fan Mountain without stopping within 4 hours. Whilst carrying out this arduous task they are also required to carry with them a 40lb

Bergen and rifle. Learn to love your Bergen! What makes this task so difficult is that they are on their own with no assistance or encouragement. The SAS will not abandon the task because of torrential rain, sleet or snow. The task must be carried out and completed within a set timeframe regardless of the conditions. To complete this successfully takes a very special type of person. Not only is it physically unbearable, but the mental fatigue on a candidate's mind is something they will have never experienced before.

PHASE 1 – WEEK 2

At the beginning of the second week you will begin the first of up to six hard testing treks across the Brecon Beacons. This is where the hard work really begins and those people who are left will begin to see the light at the end of the tunnel. It is important not to become complacent with your performance so far as the first week is relatively easy compared to what is about to come. You will feel tired and drained at this point and this is where your mental attitude is just as important as your physical fitness and stamina.

At the beginning of each day you will board a truck and be driven off to various starting locations around the Beacons. There will be a series of timed hikes during the second week, where you will have to carry a Bergen weighing up to 40lb along with your rifle. The hikes get progressively harder as you progress through the week. At the beginning of each hike your Bergen will be weighed and, if it is below weight, bricks will be added until the specified weight is reached.

It is important to pack your Bergen with the right items (see Insider tip number 8) as this can save you valuable time on the treks. The last thing you want is to be searching for an important item that you have packed incorrectly. Make

sure you fill yourself up with the right sort of calories on the morning of each trek in order to give yourself plenty of much needed energy. It may seem obvious but also make sure you visit the toilet and empty your bowels! Taking a dump during treks is ok but it will just add time to your journey. With that in mind, ensure you pack toilet roll in your Bergen, wrapped in a plastic waterproof bag.

At the beginning of each trek listen to the DS and learn to remember your grid references, as these won't be issued twice. On your way to each rendezvous point get some sleep in the back of the truck and learn to conserve energy at every opportunity.

PHASE 1 – WEEK 3

The final week of selection is termed as 'test week' and this is where all the hard work that has gone before will seem like nothing compared to what is about to come. This is the ultimate test for any soldier and the number of candidates still left for selection at this point is usually about a third. During test week candidates are required to swim across a river totally naked whilst still carrying their Bergen and rifle. It also involves a number of 24-64km marches, all over the Brecon Beacons or the Scottish Highlands, wherever the chosen terrain is. Over the years, and since the inception of the SAS selection process as it stands, a number of people have lost their lives. One of the more commonly known incidents is the tragic death of Mike Kealy in 1979. Mike Kealy was already serving in the SAS and was returning for a stint of operational duty as a Major in command of his own squadron. He was determined to prove he still had the required fitness to be an operational SAS soldier at the age of 33 and on the 1st of February 1979 he joined a batch of

SAS recruit hopefuls. He embarked on a 40-mile tab in the early hours of the morning and in treacherous conditions. The conditions were said to be so bad that you could only see a few yards in front of you due to the driving sleet, rain and snow.

This length and type of tab is extremely difficult in normal conditions let alone in the conditions that Mike faced. In total there were approximately 30 soldiers attempting the treacherous 40-mile tab that night and they all moved off from a specific point on the Beacons in two groups of fifteen. Pretty soon into the tab the two groups began to get smaller and smaller until there were a number of small groups consisting of 2-4 soldiers. However, Mike Kealy decided to go alone. Whilst this may have been surprising to many it was obvious that a current serving senior SAS officer would not want to march with a bunch of potential recruits. There was in fact no need for him to perform the 40-mile trek and the only pressure put on him to successfully complete the march came from him.

This attitude is typical of the elite SAS soldier – never shying away from any challenge and wanting to make sure he is fit enough for any mission or operation regardless of the conditions or climate. One of the problems for Major Mike Kealy was that he decided to weigh down his backpack with bricks to the weight of 55lbs instead of weighing it down with clothes and food. He did not pack sufficient waterproof clothing including a storm proof suit which is issued to the novice soldiers before each trek.

Although he did carry gloves he chose not to wear them. As soon as he started the tab he began to lose essential body heat through his soaking clothes and it wasn't long before his condition began to deteriorate. A number of novice

soldiers on the trek decided to veer off the normal path due to the deteriorating weather conditions in search of some shelter and they noticed Mike Kealy carrying on along the treacherous route in the driving sleet and rain. After about an hour into the trek Kealy needed help and a number of novice soldiers offered him this, which he refused. Further assistance was offered in the form of gloves and a storm proof suit but again Kealy refused to accept any help. It wasn't until 7 hours into the trek, at approximately 09:30 hours, that a Captain and Corporal who were also taking part in the trek noticed Kealy slumped in the snow. They managed to locate a faint pulse in his neck and they immediately dug a snow hole to afford him some protection from the elements. The Corporal provided Kealy with a sleeping bag and then began to provide first aid and warmth from his own body heat whilst the Captain went off in search of help. It took a further two hours before the alarm was raised at the Brecon Police Station at approximately 13:55 hours. The Police never became involved in the search and rescue mission, nor did the mountain rescue team, as the SAS insisted that the military authorities would deal with the incident, something that was later criticised by the Coroner acting in the investigation into Kealy's death. Eventually, some 19 hours after the Captain and the Corporal first noticed him, Kealy's body was airlifted by Helicopter off the mountain.

The SAS standard operating procedures dictate that they only move at night. Therefore, it is imperative that any potential SAS recruit is capable of moving at night under difficult conditions. During the tabs, those on selection have to keep up with the DS (Directing Staff) and anyone who is lagging behind will receive a warning. After that first warning there will be no more and a soldier will then be returned to unit.

There are usually 5 intense and difficult hikes during the third week. These vary greatly from course to course but the following gives an idea of what those on selection have to go through:

- 2 x 25km marches on the Brecon Beacons whilst carrying a 55lb Bergen.

- An intense 'heavy drag', which involves a 15-mile march across the Beacons whilst carrying a Bergen of up to 50lbs, and then an additional heavy weight of some description.

- The 'Long Drag' involves a 40-mile hike across the Brecon Beacons whilst carrying a 55lb Bergen and rifle. This must be completed in 24 hours.

Many people drop out during the third week for obvious reasons. Not only do they have to endure the long and re-lentless distances, but they have to also tackle the elements. Soldiers who have successfully passed this phase of the selection process often describe it as the hardest thing they have ever had to go through. On paper the selection process may not seem much but when you are the one going through it day in, day out and night after night, it soon takes its toll.

THINGS TO CONSIDER DURING PHASE 1 SELECTION

During selection you will be under constant assessment. Whilst this may not come as a surprise, there are a few important factors to consider that can all go a long way to helping you improve your scores and increase your chances of success.

1. It is possible to successfully complete the entire selection process yet still fail. If the SAS recruitment staff dislike

you, then you will not be joining them, no matter how fit or intelligent you are. The best way to approach selection is to do as you're told, listen carefully to all instructions, and keep your head down. Do not try to stand out from the rest of the candidates during selection, but rather aim to complete each test with high marks without licking arse, showing off or bringing undue attention to yourself.

2. Listen very carefully to everything you are being told. The Directing Staff will provide you with orders every day, which you must listen to, and follow strictly. You will notice that the DS appear to be rather relaxed about the whole process and they will give the impression that they do not care whether you pass or fail. Whilst this is true they are still watching you very carefully and will be constantly feeding back to their superiors on everything they see and hear. They will be asked their opinion about your performance, so stay focused and follow every instruction. For example, whilst on the Brecon Beacons you will be required to make your way to a number of checkpoints. When you arrive at the checkpoint listen to what the DS say, as they will only tell you once. If you fail to listen to the information provided you could find yourself without a new grid reference to make your way to.

3. The SAS selection process is extremely tough, as you already know. However, it is important to maintain a positive attitude and presence throughout. The SAS are looking for people who can successfully pass each stage of the process yet still be fresh and ready for more action. If you complete a tab or section of the selection process and are on your knees, exhausted and can no longer go any further, then you are no use to anyone. Yes, you will feel absolutely shattered and exhausted at times during the process, but always try to stand up straight, look as smart as possible, be focused and ready for more.

4. Make sure your map reading skills are exceptional and you are familiar with the terrain used during selection. Spend some time on the hills using your map and compass practising your navigation skills. If you are poor at map reading and navigation you will find yourself following other groups in the hope that they know where they're going. Do not rely on other people but have confidence in your own abilities.

5. Blisters are generally caused by friction between the skin and another surface, whether it is your socks, your boots or a combination of the two. Before we look at how to prevent and treat blisters consider the following points:

- Do your boots fit correctly and are they wide enough, deep enough and long enough to accommodate your feet comfortably?

- Are your laces secured tightly enough to prevent your feet from moving around inside your boots?

- Kick the heel of your foot back against the boot heel before lacing them up.

- Try wearing two pairs of thin socks rather than one pair of thick socks so that the friction occurs between the layers of socks rather than under the foot.

- If your feet sweat more than normal then this can increase the chance of blisters. Make sure you keep your feet clean and dry whenever possible. Foot care should be an important part of your preparation. During selection there is a strong possibility that you'll encounter blisters. As you already know, blisters are excruciatingly painful so during your preparation, and before you attend selection, you should learn how to deal with them, but more importantly take precautions to prevent them from happening in the first place.

Hill walkers, especially in the early days of their walking career, will encounter blisters. However, after a few tough walks in a pair of suitably fitting 'worn in' boots the skin will harden and the blisters will appear less frequently. This should be one of your aims during your preparation time - to harden the skin and experience the blisters before you attend selection. The only way to achieve this is to get out there training, both in the form of running and fast walking on rough terrain whilst carrying weight.

Once a blister heals, the skin will harden and the chance of you getting a blister in the same area again will be unlikely. Another way to harden your skin and help prevent blisters is to use tannic acid or tea soak. Apply a 10% mixture of tannic acid to your feet or soak them in tea soak at least twice a day for a 3-week period prior to selection.

If you do experience blisters during selection then here's what to do:

If you suspect a blister may be about to appear then it needs to be treated straight away. Remove your boots or footwear and clean your feet before drying them thoroughly. Apply a special moleskin plaster to the affected area. Moleskins can be purchased from most good pharmacy stores and you should carry a few of them with you at all times whilst on the hills. Once you have stopped walking remove the special moleskin, clean and dry the affected area and allow the air to get to it. This will aid the recovery process. Before you set off again the following day make sure you apply a fresh moleskin plaster once more.

Treating severe blisters

If the blister is filled with fluid then you should take a sterilised needle or sharp blade and pierce the blister close to the base/side, allowing the fluid to drain away. If the skin is still

intact then do not remove it, as it will provide protection for the blister as it recovers. Now cover the affected area with a clean/fresh moleskin plaster.

During selection you may come across a time when you have to either run or trek with a painful blister. Unfortunately this is all part of selection and it will be up to you to fight through the pain and continue on your way. The most effective tool you have against blisters is to use the weeks and months building up to selection wisely. During this time you should take steps to prevent blisters from occurring.

6. Whatever exercise you are taking part in, whether it is a 20-mile hike, orienteering exercise, swim, the Fan Dance or one of the endurance marches, try to finish in a good time and near to the front of the group. If you are completing an exercise in a group, then try to finish near the front. Whilst the SAS do not like a show off, they do like to see someone complete each section of the course with energy to spare and in a position that is somewhere that is near to the front of the pack. The only way you can achieve this is through high levels of fitness and determination.

7. This is the most obvious, yet most ignored tip of all. During SAS selection you will notice four different types of people:

- Those who are there as an escape from their normal posting;

- Those that are ill-prepared;

- Those that are there for the bravado and macho element so they can say 'I went through SAS selection';

- Those that are well prepared, focused and keep their heads down.

It doesn't take much to work out which category you need to

fall into. Surprisingly, this category is the least represented on selection. Do not draw unnecessary attention to yourself and do not arse lick the Directing Staff. Failure on the course can come as a result of many different things – your actions, what you say, your attitude, laziness, a lack of preparation or a simple dislike for you by one of the DS will all have you returned to unit.

Once a soldier has completed phase 1 of selection, they will then undergo a further 2 stages as follows.

PHASE 2 SELECTION – JUNGLE TRAINING

During phase 2 of the SAS selection the soldier will learn the skills that are required to become a competent member of the Regiment. This will include training in weapons, standard operating procedures, jungle training, parachuting, patrolling, and escape and evasion training. All members of the SAS must be able to swim competently and also dive. The squadron will teach a soldier how to do these competently during continuation training. The SAS operate to a number of Standard Operating Procedures (SOPs). Whilst they are a set of rules, they are also there as a safety net and also as a method for ensuring that everyone adheres to the same principles. During this stage of selection a soldier will learn the SOPs inside out and he will spend many hours learning them and putting them into practice.

Jungle Training
Jungle training will take place deep within the heart of the jungle in Belize. This territory is largely familiar to soldiers of the Parachute Regiment who make up a large proportion of SAS soldiers.

During this stage of the selection process soldiers will have to learn the basics of surviving in these difficult conditions.

In addition to surviving they will also have to carry out numerous arduous patrols in a four-man team for a total of 4 weeks. They will also be provided with limited rations. The purpose of this phase is to determine who is capable of looking after themselves and their kit whilst living and operating with three other members of the team. This type of testing places untold mental pressure on an individual in addition to the physical pressure. During this type of assessment a candidate's ability to get on with the rest of the team is under scrutiny. Imagine living in such conditions for 4 weeks with somebody whom you don't particularly get on with. Their annoying habits will soon begin to take their toll on you. However, it is essential that candidates continue to stay focused on their goal of maintaining their place in the elite force of the SAS.

PHASE 3 SELECTION – ESCAPE & EVASION INCLUDING TACTICAL QUESTIONING (TQ)

The nature of SAS operations means that soldiers and teams will often be working behind enemy lines. Therefore the risk of being captured is quite high. The SAS want to recruit soldiers who have the ability escape and evade capture and also resist any interrogation. For this phase of the course, the remaining candidates are given brief instructions on relevant techniques. This will usually involve talks with ex prisoners of war or current serving soldiers who have experience in this field. Once soldiers on this phase of the course have been briefed they are then let loose into the countryside, where they will have to escape capture from other soldiers for a three day period. Those who are caught are then taken in for tactical questioning. If a soldier is skilled enough to escape capture he will still have to endure the difficult TQ anyway once the three day period is up.

During tactical questioning each soldier is put through a very difficult period of intense interrogation. This will include being treated roughly by the interrogators whilst stood in awkward positions, often naked, cold and hungry. The interrogators will use a series of techniques to attempt to break down a candidate's determination. They will use 'white noise' in an attempt to disorientate the candidate and act in a friendly manner, again, in an attempt to get some information out of them. On the other hand they may be verbally abusive and shout extremities about a candidate's mother or girlfriend in an attempt to antagonise them. If the candidate breaks, then they will fail the whole course. They are briefed only to answer any questions with their name, rank, service number and date of birth. Any other questions should be answered with *"I'm sorry, I cannot answer that question"*. Days and days of harsh interrogation will take its toll on any soldier. The SAS are looking for men who can withstand such treatment long enough so that the effects of revealing any operational information they might have can be reduced.

Once a soldier has completed all 3 phases of selection, he will then be awarded with the much coveted beige beret. At the commencement of selection there will be approximately 125 soldiers. Out of those 125, only 10 will be selected. The soldier will then continue on an intense period of Continuation Training. The SAS have found from experience that it takes one type of person to make it through the selection process and another to become a fully competent soldier in the regiment. It is possible for a soldier to be fit enough to pass every stage of the process and training but subsequently lack the intelligence to operate effectively.

It takes approximately two years to fully train a newly recruited SAS soldier. During this time the soldier will go through many tests, both physically and mentally, in an attempt to prove

his worthiness of staying with the regiment. During the two-year training/probationary period each of the new recruits will start off by learning very basic infantry techniques. Many of them will already be specialists in their field and will have to master the basics in order to become a fully competent SAS soldier. There are a number of different sections of the regiment that a soldier can opt to specialise in as follows

- Free Fall Parachuting – Air Troop

- Mountain Troop

- Boat Troop

- Mobility Troop

Free Fall Parachuting – Air Troop

This area of specialisation will require intense Parachute training and the majority of soldiers who opt for this field have been members of the Parachute Regiment. During specialisation training they will have to learn the HALO (High Altitude - Low Opening) technique, which requires them to freefall from 25,000 feet into a tight ravine whilst loaded to the hilt with equipment and ammunition. They will also learn the HAHO (High Altitude – High Opening) technique.

Predominantly, the soldiers who form the Air Troop are specialists in airborne insertion methods. The Air Trooper uses the two techniques (HALO and HAHO) to perform infiltration. HALO jumps involve the Air Trooper freefalling until he reaches approximately 2,000 feet, when he will open his chute. The reason for this method is so that he can get very close to a target without being seen. The HALO and HAHO techniques are extremely dangerous manoeuvres due to the often heavy weights carried by the trooper, which can cause the chute to collapse in the thin air.

The Air Trooper will also wear an oxygen mask and goggles, which are both attached to his helmet whilst he is parachuting from high altitudes. The Trooper's equipment is usually carried between his legs and can be lowered on a cord just prior to him hitting the ground. In addition to this the Trooper will carry an 'altimeter' on his wrist so that correct chute opening can be executed. Due to the severe cold often experienced at high altitudes, he will wear sufficient clothing to provide adequate protection. Unlike the more conventional parachutist, the Air Trooper will carry a reserve chute on the front of his body.

MOUNTAIN TROOP

Those who specialise in this area will learn to climb on rock and ice of any formation so that they are available for such missions anywhere in the world. The SAS Mountain Troops are trained to survive and fight in extreme conditions. They often train in various different professional climbing schools, for example on the Alpine Guides course, where they reach a level of competence that rivals the most proficient climbers in the world. The Mountain Troop is highly skilled in the following areas:

Climbing cliffs and rock faces

This involves the SAS troopers being connected by a rope and other specialist equipment. Pairs of SAS climbers wear harnesses whilst they scale a rock face carrying their equipment and weapons. As they scale the rock face the climbers will place wedges and other forms of protective equipment into the cracks in the rock. The rope is hooked to these pieces of protection so that if a climber falls, the rope will catch him. However, the troopers are so highly skilled that the chance of them falling is extremely remote.

Arctic survival techniques

Surviving in artic conditions takes immense skill, training and pre-planning. One of the biggest problems faced by the SAS Mountain Troop whilst operating in the Arctic is that of navigation.

Navigation in such conditions is exactly the same as 'normal temperature' navigation apart from the added problems brought by whiteout, the change in terrain formation due to snow, pace and distance estimation whilst travelling on skis, and also the difficulty in handling navigation equipment. Due to 'whiteout', and also the difficulties in travelling at night, the SAS will estimate distances travelled by using a number of simple yet highly effective methods. A length of rope will be measured to a set distance (e.g. 50 metres). The same rope will then be tied at each end to a man. One man will ski or walk the length of the rope until the 50-metre rope becomes taught. Then, the second man will walk 100 metres until the rope once again becomes taught. Each time the rope becomes taught, 50 metres will have been travelled. This is a slow, yet effective method for calculating distances travelled whilst operating in these conditions.

Setting up a secure camp is a discipline that the Mountain Troop is highly trained in. The camp construction is carried out with the minimum of noise and disturbance so as to not give away their location to the enemy. All vehicles and equipment are hidden under trees and other forms of camouflage until nothing can be seen, yet the troop is still ready for operational deployment at a moment's notice. Shelters and dugouts are created and weapon racks constructed before the troop finally lay mines and trip flares to provide immediate notification of enemy insertion. Each tent that is erected will require a lookout and these will be changed periodically dependant on the climate conditions. Basically the colder it

is, the more often the sentries are changed. If an enemy is seen approaching, or there is cause for concern, the alarm is raised by the tugging of a string or a thin rope that is securely attached to each tent. By tugging the rope the lookout is able to immediately alert the remainder of the troop.

BOAT TROOP

The Boat Troop is responsible for all different forms of water insertion tactical operations, which include swimming, diving and canoeing. The Boat Troop train most of the time with the Special Boat Service (SBS), which is also based at Hereford. The Boat Troop, along with the SBS, is trained in the use of Klepper canoes, Gemini inflatables and other small boat craft.

During training, SAS Boat Troop members are taught how to dive correctly using Open and Closed circuit breathing devices. One of the difficult tasks the Boat Troop learns during their training is how to attach a limpet mine to a ship whilst it is on the move – something that takes immense skill and courage. The main form of transportation used by the troop is the Klepper folding kayak. The Klepper kayak has been in use for many years and was designed for use by the SAS and the Royal Marines during WWII.

The SAS Boat Troop also uses fast patrol boats that are constructed from a fibreglass hull, which allows for greater manoeuvrability and buoyancy. In addition to the dangerous act of attaching limpet mines to boats, the Boat Troop is also trained in the technique of 'locking out' of submarines. Locking out is a term used to describe a technique where a diver leaves a submarine through an air lock, in order to enter the water below surface level. This type of insertion

technique is used when the troop need to board a ship or oilrig in order to carry out a mission. When performing this type of operation, the Boat Troop will usually wear dry suits in order to protect them from hypothermia and the effects of the cold. The Boat Troop is also highly trained in underwater navigation techniques. The risk of becoming lost at sea in the dark and the cold is high. Therefore, each member of the Boat Troop will be highly competent in the skill of underwater navigation using a compass.

Methods of Navigating Underwater
Divers navigate underwater in two ways - dead reckoning and pilotage.

Dead Reckoning
This is a technique used where a diver follows a compass bearing in a specific direction, usually keeping track of speed and time. Certain factors, however, will limit the absolute accuracy of the underwater dead reckoning. The current, a variation in a diver's swimming technique, and errors in holding a course will cause the diver's 'actual' track to differ from the diver's dead reckoning.

Pilotage
This is a technique used by divers to navigate by reference to specific terrain features, both natural and artificial. The method usually requires the assistance of a chart to aid navigation. The diver who utilises the pilotage technique will follow bottom contours, gullies, reefs and kelp borders etc. This type of method should only be employed where the diver has clear visibility.

MOBILITY TROOP

The Mobility Troop predominantly specialise in a variety of

insertion methods. The vehicles they use range from the Land Rover through to motorbikes. SAS members who specialise in this field are highly trained in the maintenance of vehicles, land navigation and professional driving skills.

The Mobility Troop dates back to World War II and they are still used for the same type of mission, which includes insertion deep behind enemy lines. Mobility Troop members of the Service are highly trained mechanics that can solve mechanical problems whilst under extreme pressure. Try to think along the lines of a Formula One team mechanic and you are beginning to get the idea of the type of skills and abilities they have. Many of the Mobility Troop members are ex Royal Electrical and Mechanical Engineers (REME) types who have excelled in their field. The vehicles used within the Mobility Troop also carry a variety of weapons such as the Browning machine gun, General Purpose Machine Guns (GPMGs), Anti-Tank weapons and grenade launchers. The troop will also use high powered Quad Bikes and what is known as a 'Light Strike Vehicle' or LSV as it is otherwise called. The LSV is a simple two-seater type buggy predominantly used in desert conditions and can carry a variety of different weapons.

The Mobility Troop usually trains in the deserts of the Gulf.

THE ANTI-TERRORIST UNIT

It is worthwhile dedicating a small section of this guide to the Anti-Terrorist Unit as many members of the Squadron form part of it. As we are all aware, today's society is laden with the ever-increasing threat from terrorists.

The Anti-Terrorist unit predominantly consists of four elements:

- The Assault team

- The Long Range Sniper team

- The Command Support team

- The Communication team

Whilst the unit comprises of these four different elements they still operate as one team. Each team will train individually and also as a whole unit. They will use a number of different training venues and facilities across the UK where real life scenarios can be reconstructed in order to provide the most effective training. One of these training venues is the Fire Service College, Moreton-in-Marsh. Located in the heart of the Cotswolds it boasts such facilities as a training ship, an oilrig and many different aircraft types. This is an ideal venue for the team to hone their skills. Having personally spent a total of 12 months at the Fire Service College, I have been fortunate enough to witness the unbelievable skills of the SAS in training.

The first Anti-Terrorist Unit was set up following the Munich Olympic Games massacre and in response to the increasing threat from worldwide terrorist groups. During any terrorist event that occurs within the UK the responsibility rests with the civil authorities such as the Police. The SAS will only be brought into action if the situation is so serious that the need to prevent the further loss of life is present. In order for the SAS to take control, the Police must provide a written request at the scene to the Commander in Chief of the military.

Anti-Terrorist Unit members usually wear a black one-piece suit that is constructed of a fire resistance material.

CHAPTER 5
INSIDER TIPS AND ADVICE

INTRODUCTION

Within this section of the guide I have provided you with 10 important tips to follow during the build up to selection, and also whilst under selection. This list is not the be all and end all and you will find many other hints, tips and advice within this guide to assist you. However, the tips contained on the following pages are very important and therefore should not be neglected.

INSIDER TIP NUMBER 1
FOCUS ON YOUR GOAL (DESIRE)

Those who fail selection do so for a number of reasons, which range from either a lack of fitness, a lack of determination, being disliked by the instructors, being cocky or over-confident, not listening to the instructors, not doing what they are told, or simply giving in. All of the above are as a result of one thing – failing to focus on the ultimate goal, which is

to pass SAS selection. Remember at the commencement of the guide how I spoke about desire, and the determination to join the SAS. Both of these are crucial to a candidate's success. The problem is, these cannot be bought or simply turned on whenever required. You either have the desire and determination, or you don't. I can remember when I applied to join the Fire Service. I wanted it more than anything in the world and I trained extremely hard for it. I ran, ran some more, lifted weights, swam, learnt about the Fire Service, ran some more, ate the right food and eventually breezed the selection process. This wasn't down to luck; it was down to my sheer hard work, desire, perseverance and determination.

SAS selection is tough and there is certainly no secret formulae to succeeding. Your focus should begin months in advance of selection. Preparing yourself both mentally and physically is the key to your success. How badly you want this is down to you and nobody else. The first step to passing the selection process is in your preparation. Its pointless turning up for selection having only carried out one month's worth of preparation. If you are determined to be successful then you will focus on your goal many months prior to your selection start date. Keeping a constant focus on your goal will enable you to condition your mind to what you want to achieve.

INSIDER TIP NUMBER 2
FITNESS PREPARATION

This is an obvious tip but one that many people who are up for selection fail to take seriously. Your fitness levels prior to, and during selection, are immensely important. Before you attend selection you will have a good idea of what lies ahead, therefore you have the advantage of knowing how to prepare effectively for it. Even if you don't have a selection

date yet, you already know that the SAS run their selection process twice a year. Therefore there is nothing preventing you from starting your preparation right now.

Your fitness training programme should involve a number of different disciplines. Do not make the mistake of simply going out on a number of 'long runs'. You must include a variety of different exercises, each with varying intensity, duration and repetitions, in order to condition your body for the selection process. A varied exercise programme will improve your fitness, strength and stamina far more effectively than one that is monotonous and single tier. Variety, in terms of the different exercises utilised and the intensity of each training session is the key to your success. Concentrate on the following exercises in particular:

Running

Brisk walking/jogging with heavy weight

Swimming

Cycling

Bleep test

Indoor rowing

Press-ups

Sit-ups

Pull-ups or heaves

Star jumps

INSIDER TIP NUMBER 3
GET TO KNOW AND UNDERSTAND THE TERRAIN THAT IS USED FOR SELECTION

The majority of routes you will endure during selection will be on the Brecon Beacons, which are located in Mid Wales. However, the SAS have been using the Scottish Highlands

in more recent years as the preferred terrain for selection. Whichever area they use, get to know the terrain beforehand. The route marches and treks will probably be the toughest thing you will ever experience in your life. Therefore, being familiar with the territory prior to selection is a positive step. Do not get hung up on trying to identify specific routes that you think the SAS will use during selection, but rather get used to the surroundings, the terrain and the inclement weather conditions.

The Brecon Beacons are a lovely place during the summer months but can be treacherous during winter and the cold seasons. As detailed within this guide a number of soldiers have already lost their lives on the Beacons and the more familiar you are with the surroundings and more prepared you are in terms of map reading, fitness and equipment selection, the safer you will be. This in turn will increase your chances of success; increase your confidence, and also increase your ability to pass each test. It is advised that you spend at least two weekends walking around the Brecon Beacons to familiarise yourself with the territory and surroundings. The Beacons cover a total area of 1347 sq km (520 sq miles) so you will never be able to predict the exact routes used by the SAS during selection. However, having an understanding of the area's layout and terrain will help you during selection. Before you visit the Beacons purchase yourself the Ordnance Survey Map of the area. The map you need is OS Landranger160 and this can be purchased online. The map scale is 1:50000 (2 cm to 1 km, 1¼ inches to 1 mile), which is usually the same as the one issued to you during selection. Familiarity, both with the Beacons and the map for the area, is good preparation and it will go a long way to helping you succeed.

INSIDER TIP NUMBER 4
MAP READING COMPETENCE

If you are poor at map reading then you will struggle during selection. The majority of candidates who arrive for selection will not have read a map for many months and they will soon feel the pressure. Map reading is just as important as your fitness and when taking part in the many treks of the endurance phase you will be constantly using your map and compass. Spend plenty of time learning the basics of map reading and if the opportunity of refresher training exists within your unit, then take it up. If you decide to spend time on the Brecon Beacons, as recommended in tip number 3, you will be able to try out your map reading skills and put them to the test. Most maps used by the British Army, including the SAS, are of scale 1:50000. During selection there are a number of important things to remember and within this section we will look at them individually:

TAKING CARE OF YOUR MAP

Your map is your lifeline to where you want to be and therefore it is important that you look after it and protect it from the elements. One thing that is drilled home to you during selection is that your map must never be marked or written on for any reason. If you were on a mission with the SAS and your map became lost or captured it could give away useful information to the enemy. How you fold your map too is also important, ensuring that you do not create any further 'creases' in addition to the map's original ones. Once again this can give away information to the enemy and must be avoided at all costs. During selection, and whilst on the Brecon Beacons, your map should be protected in a suitable waterproof bag and properly sealed to prevent water making its way in.

You will be tasked with completing many long distance treks. During these treks you will come across a number of different 'checkpoints', which are manned by the Directing Staff. They will ask you details about where you have been before telling you where you are going next. Make sure you listen to what they are telling you, as they will not repeat the information. Being able to concentrate whilst under extreme pressure is all part of the selection criteria.

READING YOUR MAP

Any soldier who puts himself up for SAS selection should be a competent map reader. However, there are still a number of useful and simple tips that can help you increase your timings during selection. Simplicity and repetition is the key, or in other words, keep your map reading simple and repeat the same process every time you refer to your map.

First, you need to determine your bearing (the direction you want to travel). Use the following procedure to obtain an exact travel direction towards your desired destination. The procedure will work if the magnetic North-South lines are drawn on the map.

STEP 1
> Place the compass on the map so that the long edge connects the starting point with the desired destination.

> Make sure that the direction arrows are pointing from the starting point to the place of destination (and not the opposite way).

STEP 2
> Hold the compass firm on the map in order to keep the base plate steady.

> Turn the rotating capsule until the North-South lines on the bottom of the capsule are parallel with the North-South lines on the map.

> Be sure that the North-South arrow on the bottom of the capsule points to the same direction as North on the map.

STEP 3

> Hold the compass in your hand in front of you. Make sure that the base plate is in the horizontal position, and that the direction arrows are pointing straight ahead.

> Rotate your body until the North-South arrow on the bottom of the capsule lines up with the magnetic needle, and the red end of the needle points in the same direction as the arrow.

> The directional arrows on the base plate will now show your desired travel direction.

Now that you have determined your necessary bearing, you need to make sure you maintain an accurate bearing. First, you should find a suitable target in the distance (e.g. a tree, bush or other suitable landmark) towards which the direction arrows point. Walk towards the chosen object without looking at your compass. When you reach your target, find a new object that is aligned with your bearing, and repeat the process.

TIP: Sometimes the compass capsule may get turned accidentally while you are walking. Remember to check from time to time that the capsule has not deviated from the direction that had been set on the compass. You will be using a prismatic compass during selection which will normally have the facility to tighten or lock the bezel when it is not being turned.

HOW TO LOCATE A GRID REFERENCE

All Ordnance Survey maps (and the majority of others) contain vertical and horizontal grid lines known as Eastings and Northings. If the lines, which are light blue in colour, were to be drawn on the ground, they would be exactly one kilometre apart.

On the map itself, the grid lines are 4cms apart on the 1:25000 scale and 2cms apart on the 1:50000 scale. The grid numbers on the east-west or horizontal axis are called the Eastings, and the grid numbers on the north-south or vertical axis are called the Northings. When a grid reference is provided the Eastings always come first. For example, take a look at the following map section:

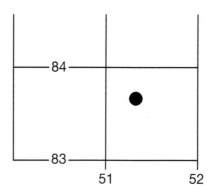

Grid references are usually indicated by a 6-figure number.

The black dot indicated on the diagram above is located at grid reference 513837. Remember that the Eastings are provided first, which in this instance are '513'. The '51' identifies the grid in which the black dot is located and the '3' indicates that the black dot is 3/10ths along the grid.

The same rule applies for the '837' of the grid reference; only the difference this time is that these three numbers are referring to the Northings. In this instance the '83' refers to the location of the black dot in the grid and the '7' indicates that the black dot is 7/10ths up the grid.

STAYING ON TRACK

There is a good possibility that you will lose your direction during phase 1 whilst tabbing, especially during the middle of the night and also during poor weather conditions. You will need to complete the majority of treks and tabs under a specific time limit and apart from your fitness levels there are other ways to improve your timings. One of them is having the ability to understand where you are going without having to constantly refer to your map and compass. The most effective method for reducing your timings is to take your reading and then focus on a prominent point, object or landmark, as far in the distance as possible that is also visible on the map. Then, have the confidence to progress to that point without checking your map or compass. Once you reach the landmark then take a further reading and repeat the process.

FINDING YOUR WAY WITHOUT THE USE OF A COMPASS

There may be times during selection where you will need to find your way without the aid of a compass. The majority of candidates on selection are competent in 'way finding' without the aid of their compass. However, for those who are not competent, here are a few tips and hints to help you:

The Shadow-Tip Method
1. To begin with you will need to find a straight stick of thin

branch approximately 1 metre in length. Place the stick upright into the ground so that you can see its shadow. Make sure the surface you have placed the stick into is as flat as possible.

2. Now mark the tip of the shadow using a suitable object such as a small stick or stone. Make sure you take the time to mark it as accurately as possible.

3. Now wait for approximately 10-15 minutes. The shadow will move from west to east in an arc.

4. Now mark the new position of the shadow's tip with another small stick or stone. During the 10-15 minute period the shadow will only move a short distance but this should be sufficient time for you to take a reading.

5. Draw a straight line in the ground between the two marks. This line is called the 'east-west line'.

6. Finally, stand with the first mark (west) on your left, and the other (east) on your right. You are now facing approximately true north. (Accuracy improves as your location approaches the equator, and as the time of year approaches either equinox.)

Watch Method: Northern Hemisphere

Make sure that your watch (the kind with hour and minute hands) is set accurately. Now place it on a level surface, such as the ground, or you may prefer to hold it horizontal in the palm of your hand.

1. To begin with, point the hour hand at the sun. You can use a stick to cast a shadow to aid in your alignment if you wish but this is not necessary.

2. Bisect (find the centre point of) the angle between the hour hand and the twelve o'clock mark. The centre of the

angle between the hour hand and twelve o'clock mark is the north-south line. If you don't know which way is north and which is south, just remember that no matter where you are, the sun rises in the east and sets in the west. In the northern hemisphere the sun is due south at midday. If your watch is set to daylight saving time bisect the angle between the hour hand and the one o'clock mark instead.

Watch Method: Southern Hemisphere

1. Using your watch as above, point the watch's twelve o'clock mark toward the sun again. If your watch is set to daylight saving time, point the one o'clock mark toward the sun.

2. Bisect the angle between the twelve o'clock mark (or one o'clock mark if using daylight saving time) and the hour hand to find the north-south line. If you're unsure which way is north, remember that the sun rises in the east and sets in the west no matter where you are. In the southern hemisphere, however, the sun is due north at midday.

Using the Stars: Northern Hemisphere

Locate the North Star (Polaris) in the night sky. The North Star is the last star in the handle of the Little Dipper constellation as indicated below.

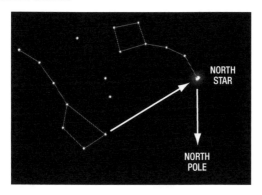

If you have trouble finding it, find the Big Dipper instead which is also indicated in the diagram. You will notice that the two lowest stars in the Big Dipper (the outermost stars of the cup of the dipper) form a straight line that 'points' to the North Star. The North Star is located about midway between the central star of Cassiopeia and the Big Dipper. Draw an imaginary line straight down from the North Star to the ground. This direction is true north, and if you can find a landmark in the distance at this point, you can use it to guide yourself.

Using the Stars: Southern Hemisphere
Find the Southern Cross constellation, which is indicated in the diagram below.

This constellation is formed by five stars, and the four brightest stars form a cross that is angled to one side.

1. Identify the two stars that make up the long axis of the cross. These stars form a line that 'points' to an imaginary point in the sky, which is above the South Pole. Follow the imaginary line down from the two stars to five times the distance between them.

2. Draw an imaginary line from this point to the ground and

try to identify a corresponding landmark to steer by. Since this is true south, true north is directly opposite it (behind you as you are looking at the point).

Moon Method

1. Observe the moon. If it is not a full moon and rises before the sun sets, the illuminated side is west. If the moon rises after midnight the illuminated side is east. This is true everywhere on Earth.

2. Approximate north and south based on the rough east-west line of the moon. No matter where you are, if you are standing with the west side to your left, true north will be straight ahead.

INSIDER TIP NUMBER 5
BE PREPARED FOR THE ELEMENTS

The time of year that you are on selection will determine the type and severity of weather conditions you will be faced with. The major problem with selection during the winter months is that there is the risk of hypothermia and frostbite. These usually occur during temperatures below freezing and with the 'night treks' that are guaranteed during selection the risk will increase.

The danger presented, in terms of frostbite and hypothermia, can be decreased if you take a number of precautions. You must take care of the areas of your body where heat is most likely to escape. These include your hands, feet, neck and head and it is important that these are covered up and kept warm as often as possible.

Early signs of frostbite include a 'pins and needles' sensation, which is often followed by numbness. Frostbitten skin will be hard, pale, cold and there may be early throbbing or

aching in the affected areas, but later on the affected part becomes insensate (devoid of feeling). When the affected area has thawed out, it becomes red and painful. With more severe frostbite, the skin may appear white and numb, which usually indicates that the tissue has started to freeze. Very severe frostbite can cause blisters, gangrene (blackened dead tissue), and damage to the deep structures such as tendons, muscles, nerves and bone can occur.

When faced with severe inclement weather conditions you will need to keep checking for signs of the above. If you suspect frostbite or hypothermia then you must take immediate action to prevent the condition from deteriorating.

Treating hypothermia

The first step for treating hypothermia is to preserve your body heat and prevent anymore from being lost. This means changing out of any wet clothing and covering up affected areas. Move out of the cold as much as possible and try to find a suitable shelter. You will find that the steep contours of the Brecon Beacons will afford you some protection from the severe wind, thus helping to reduce the wind chill factor.

If you suspect a colleague is suffering from the effects of hypothermia then you can use your own body heat to help them increase their body temperature. Hugging them or placing their hands under your armpits or in between your groin area can help transfer essential heat where it is needed the most. If possible try to eat carbohydrates, which will provide you with much needed rapid energy, or fats to provide prolonged fuel for your body. Obviously what you can eat will be determined by how much food and the type of food you are carrying in your Bergen or rucksack. Think ahead prior to the trek and pack the right foods and drinks.

Treating frostbite

The simplest and most effective way to treat frostbite is to move your fingers or toes in order to increase circulation. Do not rub or massage the area, as this can be extremely painful. Keep the whole body as warm as possible and immediately remove any wet clothing. If it is possible, gradually re-warm the area affected using warm water for approximately 30 minutes. If warm water is not available (which it won't be on the Beacons) wrap the affected area in warm clothing or a sleeping bag.

If you get lost

During the SAS selection it is unlikely that you'll get lost but there are procedures in place to rescue you if the unfortunate circumstance occurs. The main thing to remember if you do get lost is that you will be found by the search team that is sent out to rescue you. All you need to do is focus on your survival. If you do get lost the risk from hypothermia or frostbite increases, so try to understand each of the conditions and take the necessary precautions to prevent them from happening.

INSIDER TIP NUMBER 6
YOUR CLOTHING AND PERSONAL HYGIENE

During selection it is important that you take the right steps to protect yourself from the elements. One of the biggest problems you will face, especially out on the hills and Beacons, is that of wind chill. Wind chill is the apparent temperature, which describes the cooling effect on exposed skin by the combination of temperature and wind and is expressed as the loss of body heat. Increased wind speed will accelerate the loss of body heat.

A wind chill factor of -30 degrees or lower on exposed skin

will result in frostbite in a very short period of time. As an example, a 5° day with a wind speed of 15 miles per hour will feel the equivalent to a -13° day. Therefore, the precautions you take to protect yourself from wind chill are of paramount importance if you are to survive the elements during SAS selection.

Taking precautions from wind chill

The clothing that you will be supplied with by your regiment, and that you will be wearing during selection, will be of a high standard. Try to keep your clothing as clean as possible throughout selection as the dirt will deteriorate the protective qualities of the garment. At the end of each session spend time preparing your kit for the following day. It is easy to let your kit go by the wayside but always remember that the state and repair of your clothing and equipment could save your life in a survival situation.

The wet weather will always be one of your biggest problems. Again, at the end of each day make sure you dry your clothes adequately in preparation for the following day. If you do not then you will be increasing the risk of wind chill. The cold weather will just sap the heat from your body and the wet clothing will no longer act as a protective barrier to the elements. The most effective method for protecting yourself from the cold weather is the three-layer system. This is a well known, tried and tested method used by many professional hill walkers/mountaineers in their pursuit to avoid the perils of the elements.

The base layer

The three-layer system utilises a base layer, an intermediate layer and an outer layer. The base layer is the first layer of clothing you put on and it is in direct contact with your skin. During SAS selection it is very likely that you will be sweating,

cooling down, sweating, cooling down etc over prolonged periods. The base layer will enable you to cool down quickly whilst still maintaining a level of warmth and protection. One of the problems faced during any strenuous outdoor exercise is that of 'post exercise chill'. Certain clothing/material types, such as cotton T-shirts, will absorb any sweat and moisture that you produce during and following exercise. The problem with this type of material is that it will retain that cold moisture instead of transporting it away from your body. This in turn will force your body to increase its heat production and the cold, wet cotton T-shirt could cause your body to under-cool. The types of material you use as a base layer should not retain the moisture but rather transport it away from your body in order to counteract the post-exercise chill.

The Insulation Layer

The second layer of clothing, after the base layer, is known as the insulation layer. The insulation layer is the second layer of clothing, which is put on top of the base layer. The insulation layer is used to retain your body heat by means of creating a layer of dead air around your body. This dead air will have the result of decreasing the heat exchange between your body and the outside elements. The insulation layer should consist of a material that has the ability to stand up and effectively trap the air inside the fibres. Such materials are usually found in the form of fleece jackets or shirts.

The Outer Layer

The final Layer in the three-layer system is called the outer layer. This is the only layer to have direct contact with the outside elements. The outer layer is designed to:

- Protect you from the external elements such as snow, sleet and rain.

- Disperse body moisture.

Outer layers are usually waterproof and have the ability to protect you from wind chill if constructed from the right material. How waterproof the outer layer is will be dependant upon the type of material used in its construction. The breathability of the outer layer is dependant upon the size of the outer shell layer material membrane. The 'pore size' of the material used should be bigger than a water vapour molecule yet smaller than a water droplet. During 1976, Gore-Tex was developed, which is a membrane of a petrochemical polymer called polytetrafluorethylene (PTFE).

Since 1976, many different variations of Gore-Tex have been developed that fall under the category name of PTFE laminates. Gore-Tex is an ideal material for forming an outer layer of the three layer system. Using the three-layer system will give you the best possible protection from the outdoor elements that you are likely to face during the SAS selection process. In most cases, the three-layer system pertains to upper body clothing. The torso and neck area are the most important things to insulate as they protect your body core. In extremely cold conditions, however, this three-layer system can be used for full body protection and you may find this of use during selection, depending on the weather conditions you are presented with at the time.

Looking after your feet

If your feet are in poor condition then don't expect to get too far during selection. Think about it logically – if the tyres on your car are worn down and in a poor state of repair then you are likely slide around the road surface and the possibility of you getting a puncture will dramatically increase. A similar rule applies to your feet – if you protect them with wet or dirty socks and you wear the wrong boots then you will soon realise that you cannot go much further.

Throughout selection make sure your socks are clean and dry at all times and that you carry a spare pair with you in your Bergen so that you can change them whenever necessary. Remember to clean and thoroughly dry your feet first before changing your socks. Selection requires you to trek many hundreds of miles over a lengthy period across some very difficult terrain. On top of this you will be carrying heavy weights in the form of your Bergen, rifle, and sometimes ammunition boxes. Therefore the weight that is distributed to your feet greatly increases. Make sure your boots are in good condition, worn in and feel comfortable. One of the biggest mistakes you can make during selection is to arrive with a brand new pair of shining boots! Whilst you may look the smartest you will soon be sporting a number of 'selection ending' blisters.

There are a number of ways that you can increase the life of your boots and also protect them during selection. The first and most obvious method is to ensure that your boots are kept clean whenever possible. Do not simply place them under a hot running tap, but meticulously clean off the dirt and mud carefully with just enough hot water so that you don't 'over wet' your boots. Following on from this your boots should be kept dry. During selection it will be up to you to make sure your boots are kept dry.

Remember to keep bootlaces clean and dry too as constant dampness can cause them to rot. If you are out on a long trek then the last thing you need is your laces falling apart on you. Take the time to change your laces every night after returning from each trek and keep them as clean and dry as possible. Also carry a spare pair of laces with you in your Bergen just in case you need them.

All this extra time and effort spent looking after yourself and your clothing may seem to be a pain in the arse but it is definitely worth the effort. Many people on selection choose to take gaiters with them to further protect the boot from the ingress of dirt, snow and moisture. Whilst not essential you may find this to be a good option and it will save you some time cleaning and drying your boots every night. Finally, take with you a protective boot wax, which will add to the waterproofing of the footwear and help to keep your boots supple and comfortable.

INSIDER TIP NUMBER 7
BE PHYSICALLY AND MENTALLY PREPARED FOR THE ROUTE SELECTION STAGES

If you are preparing for selection then you will no doubt be aware of the route selection phase. Designed to push any man to his limits, the route selection phase is as mentally tough as it is physical. If you fail to prepare properly for this stage of selection then you will almost certainly fail.

During selection the SAS selection staff will test you relentlessly over a large number of often long and difficult timed hikes, predominantly over the Brecon Beacons. The type and distance of the routes used by the SAS varies each year in order to prevent them becoming known by the candidates who are on selection. If the routes were to remain the same then soldiers would be able to practise them prior to selection and therefore unfairly increase their chances of success.

During a separate section of this guide we made reference to the importance of familiarising yourself with the Brecon Beacons and recommend that you spend some time on them becoming accustomed to the climate and the environment.

Putting into practice your map reading skills on the Beacons is also a very important part of your preparation and it will go a long way to making you feel more at ease during the endurance stage.

INSIDER TIP NUMBER 8
LEARN TO LIVE WITH YOUR BERGEN

Carrying a Bergen, especially over long treks across rough and often difficult terrain, is an arduous task. Add 50lbs to the equation and it's even harder! During SAS selection your Bergen will become a part of you and it is important that you look after it, pack it correctly and learn to carry it using the correct technique.

Packing your Bergen

Learn to pack your Bergen carefully and methodically, taking the time to ensure that the most used and important items are easily accessible. The item you will need access to the most is your water, so therefore it should be available at all times. The last thing you want to have to do is stop to take off your Bergen each time you want a drink. Start off by creating a list of everything you intend keeping in your Bergen and tick each item off in order of priority. The lowest numbers should be packed first and placed at the bottom of the Bergen, such as your sleeping bag or spare clothing. Time spent on this important area during preparation will reduce your timings on the hills during the selection process. If you are not used to carrying a Bergen, or you are out of practice, then get some in before you attend selection. At times your Bergen will weigh 50 pounds or more so you must get used to carrying it over long periods and distances. During your time spent on the hills you will get wet so make sure everything you pack that is porous (i.e. soaks up water) is placed in plastic bags or another suitable waterproof lightweight container.

How to carry your Bergen correctly

The Bergen should be carried high up on your back so that the weight is evenly distributed and the amount of strain on your back is minimised. If you have carried out the right type of training prior to selection, and practised carrying a Bergen, then your leg muscles should be strong enough to take the load.

Before you put on your Bergen, first loosen the shoulder straps and all other tensioning straps. Put the rucksack on your back and fasten the hip belt (if relevant) so that its upper edge sits comfortably over the top of your hip bones. Finally, pull in the shoulder straps and tighten the tensioning straps to a tension point that allows freedom of movement.

INSIDER TIP NUMBER 9
BE PREPARED FOR ESCAPE & EVASION AND TACTICAL QUESTIONING

If you make it far enough through to this stage of selection then you have done extremely well. Escape & Evasion and Tactical Questioning is one of the toughest parts of selection. This cannot be over emphasised. The interrogation phase of selection does not differ from the kind of treatment that terrorist suspects complained about in Ulster during 1971, and which was studied by the Compton Commission. At the commencement of interrogation, soldiers on selection will be totally exhausted and will have already been subjected to physical hardship and sensory deprivation. This occurs in the form of a dark hood placed over the head for many hours at a time. In addition to this, white noise and psychological torture are used in an attempt to force the soldier to reveal his name and also the regiment that he is from. During a real life scenario, the aim is for the soldier to hold off giving any information away that could compromise a mission or put other people in danger. The type of person who usually fails at this stage is of no particular type – it can happen to anybody. No matter how hard you try to tell yourself that it is only part of selection, you can only feel the realness of each interrogation session and the 'realness' that those issuing out the punishment add to the situation. That said there are a number of coping techniques one can employ to ease the pain and discomfort, which we will discuss later.

Those who have successfully passed selection have previously stated that they were interrogated for different lengths of time, which included an intense half-hour period, an eight-hour period and finally a 24-hour period. The SAS will use white noise, bright electric lights, flashing lights, shackles, chains, dogs and other methods in their attempts

to make you crack. There have been times when candidates have been secured to a wooden plank and placed under water for a number of seconds, once again to try to break them. This method, from an interrogator's point of view, works well. Even though the candidate knows that the interrogators are not trying to drown him, there will always be that fear that things could go wrong. It is at this point that many candidates give in. An SAS interrogator will also use other fear tactics in order to make you break. Whilst being interrogated in one room, candidates can often hear another person being beaten in a separate room along with the cries for help and also the sound of vomiting.

Whilst these are only being acted out by the interrogators, they are enough to put considerable added strain on an already tired soldier. Probably one of the most frightening of experiences used by the SAS in the past is that of a railway line and a train. Candidates are placed blindfolded on a track and handcuffed to the rail. A member of the interrogation team will shout out that a train is approaching nearby and a frantic rush ensues as they try to locate the keys to unlock the candidates. Of course they find the keys and the train that is approaching is on a separate line close by. The wise candidates place their hands either side of the track with the handcuff chain braced over the line hoping that the train will break the chain and they can escape. Unsurprisingly many candidates break at this point and shout for the interrogators to release them.

Another method used by the interrogation team is to leave candidates out in the cold totally naked. A woman is used as part of the team and will make jokes about the size of a candidate's penis, which will have shrunk due to the cold weather! Very embarrassing for most men but for the candidate who is totally focused on his aim this will not deter

him in the slightest. Women interrogators are also used as part of a 'softening' approach. Men respond differently to women, who can have more persuasive powers when used in the right manner. This type of approach will also have the effect of confusing the candidate who is under interrogation and they can often crumble under the pressure.

In a real life interrogation situation a soldier is likely to need skills of evasion in the following situations:

- When escaping from a POW camp (Prisoner of War);

- When he becomes lost from his troop during a mission;

- When escaping from a situation when he and his troop are surrounded, either as a team or on his own.

If you are captured then it is a requirement of law that the capturing body informs a protection power such as the Red Cross. This is the only reason for providing your captor with your name, rank, number and date of birth. It is highly unlikely that your captors will actually inform the protection power, especially if you are captured by a terrorist unit.

How to behave during capture and interrogation
One of the first and most important things to remember if you are captured is to remain calm. Easier said than done, but anything other than this will give your captor the impression that you are willing to assist them and provide them with information. This will have the detrimental effect of prolonging the interrogation.

The best form of behaviour is to keep in the background as much as possible and only speak if spoken to. Do not be rude or try to antagonise the interrogator. Be polite and courteous but do not shout or become aggressive, no matter how much you want to. The British Armed Forces are

renowned worldwide for their professionalism and conduct and the interrogator will know this from the offset. If he/she gets the feeling that you are unlikely to break then this will work in your favour. An interrogator will want to know how intelligent you are and he will get a good indication of this from your attitude. If you tell him to 'piss off' when being asked a question he will feel the aggression within you and see this as a weakness that he can attack and break down. If you are polite and calm the interrogator will have his work cut out and he will be aware of this.

One of the first steps used by a skilled interrogator is the 'softening up' technique. This can be achieved in a number of ways including rough treatment, sleep deprivation, solitary confinement or alternatively an attempt to get you on side. He may offer you food and warm drinks, gifts, cigarettes and even a plane back home to your family. If you are placed in solitary confinement, which is highly likely, then do not become afraid. Focus on your goal and try remembering the reason why you are there. Remember that the longer the interrogation and bad treatment goes on, the weaker you will become. If you know this then you will be far better placed to deal with it.

Interrogators often use repetition techniques in order to break you. Imagine sitting in a cold dark room having to listen to a dreadful song over and over again for eight hours. This type of treatment is designed to break you down, ready for further interrogation. Added with the fact that you will be hungry and thirsty, your will and determination to beat the interrogators will be stretched to the limit. One of the most effective methods for resisting interrogation is that of a focused mind and steady breathing. You must focus your mind on a positive image or thought and keep going back to it when you feel the need. In order to achieve this

state of mind you must employ a steady and shallow breathing technique.

Concentrate on breathing in and out through your nose and try to relax your muscles. Whilst under interrogation you will feel nervous, frightened and anxious. In turn these feelings will create tension, which will waste away all of your energy. A concentrated breathing technique will help you to counteract these negative thoughts and preserve energy.

INSIDER TIP NUMBER 10
UNDERSTAND THE WEATHER

You may think I'm mad for saying this but an understanding of how the weather changes and reasons for it will help you during selection and whilst on the Brecon Beacons.

Fog

Fog and mist are both made of tiny water droplets that are suspended in the air. The main difference between the two is the density of the droplets. Fog is denser than mist and so contains more water droplets. The official definition of fog is when visibility reaches less than 1000 metres. This limit is more appropriate for aviation purposes, but for the general public and motorists an upper limit of 200 metres is a more realistic distance. However, whilst on selection you are likely to have even lower distances of vision, which will only serve to disorientate you. That's why your map reading skills are very important.

The atmosphere is made up of many different gases and one of these is water vapour. It can hold a certain amount of water as invisible water vapour at any given temperature. If air is cooled it can hold less water and becomes super saturated. At saturation point, some of the water has to condense to form water droplets, which in turn forms cloud.

There are four different types of fog in the UK: radiation fog, advection fog, hill fog and coastal fog. The type of fog you will be presented with during selection will be hill fog, depending on the time of year that you are on selection. Hill fog or upslope fog, as it is otherwise called, is formed as the mild moist air is forced to ascend a hill. As the air moves up the windward side of the mountain it cools down, and again if the air becomes saturated then a cloud is formed, which creates fog if it is below the top of the hills.

It is possible to anticipate fog when there is moisture in the air and there is a difference in temperature. Common places to find fog are in low-lying areas or deep valleys and near bodies of water. Remember that fog can collect very quickly. Light fog can rapidly become thick fog and surround you, causing navigation problems.

The change between day and night

The length of a day changes as the year progresses. This occurs because the earth spins at a tilt. If the earth did not tilt, then the days and nights would all be the same length. The length of day and night very much depends on whereabouts you are on Earth, with the extremes being at the North and South Poles.

Planet Earth rotates around a line that is approximately 23.5 degrees to the poles. The southernmost line where the sun is directly overhead is called the Tropic of Capricorn and the northernmost line is the Tropic of Cancer. Due to the tilt of planet Earth, the North Pole will sometimes point towards the sun, whilst the South Pole points away. When this situation occurs the North Pole will have 24 hours of daylight for approximately 6 months of the year, whilst the South Pole remains in total darkness. Following this, the North Pole then tilts away from the sun. On the equator line, the sun is always

nearly overhead, so therefore the days are more constant with approximately twelve hours of daylight and twelve hours of darkness each day. In the United Kingdom, the day length obviously depends on where you are. The UK is located north of the equator, in the south there is less change, but most places still have a longest day of over sixteen hours, and a shortest of under eight.

The longest day of the year is known as the summer solstice, and occurs on the 21st of June. On this particular date the sun is directly overhead at its nearest point to the UK, above the Tropic of Cancer. Conversely, the shortest day of the year is on the 21st of December, when the sun is furthest away, directly overhead at the Tropic of Capricorn. The tilt of the earth is not only responsible for the changing day lengths, but the change in seasons as well. When the Earth is tilted with the northern hemisphere pointing towards the sun, the sun's rays hit the UK more directly. A more intense sun gives days that are warmer, as well as longer. This is called summer. When the earth is tilted away from the sun, the sunlight then has to pass through more of the Earth's atmosphere before it reaches the ground. During this situation the sun is weaker. This then gives us the cold, short days of winter that we are all too familiar with in the UK.

The three mountain ranges that constitute the Brecon Beacons are fantastically green and pleasant. However, this can give a false sense of security. The weather often changes rapidly during the course of each day. This will make a big difference to your progress whilst on selection in the hills and it will also place you in greater danger. Keep an eye on the weather and listen to each brief before you set off. Mist, snow, rain and wind can quickly confuse your sense of direction.

CHAPTER 6
SAS TACTICAL QUESTIONING

SAS INTERROGATION

During the latter stages of selection, each candidate that remains will be put through an intensive period of interrogation which is known as Tactical Questioning (TQ). There is a very good reason why the selection process includes such a stage, and that is because Special Force's soldiers are often required to work deep behind enemy lines. Although the SAS are extremely highly trained, the risk of getting captured obviously increases with such territory.

This stage of selection is called 'Escape and Evasion' (E&E) and is specifically designed to see whether a candidate has the mental and physical strength to resist interrogation and questioning on a scale that is beyond the norm. Before this stage commences, each of the remaining candidates will be provided with a very slim brief. They will be told that, when they are eventually caught, they are not to disclose any information whatsoever other than their name, rank, number

and their date or birth. If they provide any further information then they will fail selection. Therefore, it is easy to see that, with trained interrogators against them, the chances of surviving this stage are extremely slim. Only those candidates with extreme strength of mind and determination will be able to survive what lies ahead of them.

Before the E&E stage commences, the remaining candidates will also receive talks from former Prisoners of War (POW's) and SAS soldiers who have been in real life interrogations. This will provide the candidate with the reassurance that it is possible to pass this stage of selection. Mental approach, mind-set and attitude are everything. The E&E stage lasts for 3 days, during which time the candidates must 'go on the run' in a secluded and wooded area. They must fend for themselves out in the wild and avoid being captured. If they are captured, then they will face a lengthy period of intense interrogation. If they are clever enough to escape capture, then they must still face interrogation after a specified time limit.

The interrogators themselves are highly trained and skilled in this area, and have an amazing array of tools and resources to break down the candidate. More often than not, it is not the shouting or white noise that breaks a candidate, but the standing in stressful positions for lengthy periods of time with little food or water.

During this section of the guide we will explore some of the techniques used by the assessors and also the tactics a candidate can use in order to get through this stage of selection.

TACTICS USED BY THE ASSESSORS

Standing in stress positions

Standing in stress positions for long periods of time, without food or water, is pure purgatory. Having to do this after spending 3 days on the run is unthinkable! However, for the soldier on selection, this is what he will have to endure. So, picture the scene, you've been on the run for 3 days and eventually you are caught. You are starving hungry, dehydrated, confused and physically exhausted. Your captors are now going to make you stand with your legs wide apart against a wall totally naked with a black bag over your head. How long can you last for before you quit? 2 hours? Maybe 6 hours? Try standing in that position for 12 hours solid with no company except your own thoughts. This is enough to drive anyone to the edge of despair.

The assessors aren't allowed to punch you or physically hurt you. But then after just reading what you've read, do you think they need to? There won't be many candidates left at this stage of selection, and those that do remain, still have it all to come.

White noise

White noise is a sound or electrical noise that has a relatively wide continuous range of frequencies of uniform intensity. In other words, it is bloody annoying! Try and think of the noise a TV will make if it is not tuned into the correct frequency. Then turn up the volume to a loud level and listen to it for an hour. You'll now have some kind of idea of how white noise is used by the SAS during the selection process in an attempt to get a candidate to crack or disclose information.

Another example of white noise used during this type of scenario is a loud noise that sounds like a woman screaming, played backwards and repeated on a short cycle so that the drone becomes repetitive and inescapable. Imagine having to listen to that for 12 hours solid. It has the potential to drive you mad. A soldier on selection who not only has to stand in stress positions for long periods of time with a black bag over his head, must try as hard as he can to block out the noise.

During experiments which entail the use of white noise it was determined that those people who sang their favourite album or sounds in their head managed sufficiently enough to detract the negative effects of white noise. Although those people used during experiments hadn't had the unfortunate experience of spending weeks on SAS selection beforehand!

Interrogation through interview

Let's assume that you've managed to last for 12 hours standing in the stress position. They come into the cold room where you've been standing for the last 12 hours, take off your black bag and then take you off to an interview room. You sit down in a chair and they give you a sandwich to eat and a glass of water. They then start their interrogation, what are you here for? You reply with name, rank, number,

date of birth. They continue to harass and question you for a two hour period. For every question that is thrown at you, you reply with the same response, but even saying that continually is starting to take its toll on your shattered mind.

Then the interviewers change tact; they bring in a young attractive woman who appears to take pity on you. She brings you in more food and water and already you can feel yourself warming to her. Potentially this is a chink in your armour. It was easy to respond with the big 4 (name, rank, number DOB) to those dickheads who were sat in front of you, but this woman is a different kettle of fish altogether. It is at this point that the soldier must remember that any deviation from the information that he is only permitted to disclose will result in failure. All of that hard work and perseverance, only to go and throw it all away because some young attractive woman is starting to take pity on your predicament. Remember, she is one of them and her job is to make you crack.

After a further 60 minutes of constant questioning they tell you that you are going back in the room that you came from for an unlimited period of time standing in the stress position with the black bag over your head. They tell you that you are staying there until you give in. They shove you back in the room, make you stand in an even more uncomfortable position, and then close the door behind you. What do you do now?

Cast your mind back to the selection process that I underwent in order to become a firefighter. Remember the hose running where I couldn't go any further? The assessor was using this method as a trick to see who would keep going and who would give in. Now I'm certainly not saying that firefighter selection is as tough as SAS selection, because is certainly isn't. But the principle behind the tactic used to see how far

you will go is exactly the same. The key to passing is to have a mind set that says you will never give in, regardless of what happens. You must keep telling yourself that you will not stop and you will not let them beat you at all costs!

CHAPTER 7

HOW TO USE A COMPASS

This may seem like a strange chapter to include in a guide that is preparing current serving soldiers to join the SAS. However, being able to competently read a compass is one of the most important elements of selection. If your compass reading skills are either rusty or poor, then you simply won't pass selection.

Apart from determining the direction of north, a compass enables you to work out a compass bearing. This skill is imperative to the soldier who is going through selection. The skill of taking a compass bearing will be used by a candidate time and time again during his stay on the Brecon Beacons or the Scottish Highlands that are used as part of phase 1 selection. A compass bearing is in effect the angle measured in number of degrees between 0 and 360. This then tells you the direction from your current position to you objective. If a soldier cannot use a map correctly and read a compass, then there is absolutely no way he will pass selection. He will either lose precious minutes on his tab, or he will become disorientated. If either or both of these occur, then he will fail.

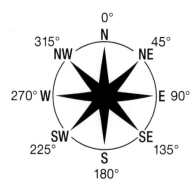

Using the above diagram we call the direction North '0' degrees. Therefore, 90 degrees is East, 180 degrees is South, 225 degrees is South West and 315 degrees is North West. If we just used the points of the compass, (north, south, east, west and so on) we would only get eight different directions (or possibly 16 or 32 at most if we further divided the compass points, for example, south-southwest or north-northeast, and so on). By using 'bearings', the soldier who is on selection can have 360, which enables him to be much more accurate. If he is accurate, then he will save much time.

Once a soldier has determined a direction (and bearing) in which to travel, he can then check his direction at regular intervals along the route or tab to confirm that he is still going in the correct direction. Although he probably won't be able to see his ultimate destination or check-point, he will have the peace of mind that he is on the right track.

WHAT IS A COMPASS?

Before we learn how to use a compass, we must first understand what one is. A compass is an instrument which includes a magnetised needle which points to magnetic north. The purpose of the compass is to determine direction

for the user. Compasses come in many different shapes and sizes and are used on land (during SAS selection), at sea or in the air.

There are many different types of compass on the market, such as the more common silva type, the simple map setting compass, and the air damped compass. However, for those people who are preparing for selection I recommend you become competent in the use of the *prismatic* compass. The prismatic compass is a compass that contains a prism which enables a bearing to be taken whilst maintaining sight of your objective. It is far more accurate than other compasses that I have mentioned but the downside is that it is harder to use. Because of this you should only the compass once the *basic* principles of map and compass work have been mastered.

THE PRISMATIC COMPASS

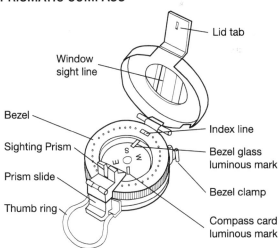

As indicated in the above diagram, the main components of the prismatic compass include:

Bezel

Sighting prism

Window sightline

Lid tab

Index line

Bezel glass luminous mark

Bezel clamp

Compass card luminous mark

Thumb ring

Prism slide

PREPARING THE COMPASS FOR USE

When using the prismatic compass it is important that you keep it as level as possible. This will ensure that any inaccuracies are kept to absolute minimum. You should also take care to make sure that any ferrous objects, such as a metal watch or knife, are kept away from the compass, otherwise this too can cause errors in the reading.

Step 1
Open up the compass lid until it stands at a 90 degree angle to the main compass body.

Step 2
Now turn the sighting prism over until the sighting slit is resting fully on the prism.

Step 3
The next step is to adjust the sighting prism. Hold the compass steadily in one hand and look through the sighting prism at the compass card gradients. With your free thumb,

push up at the base of the prism mount in order to raise the prism in its slide. Keep raising it until you see the compass card numerals in focus.

TAKING A BEARING ON OBJECTS IN THE DISTANCE

Step 1
To begin with, hold the compass as per the following diagram:

Step 2
Hold the compass approximately 2 inches from your eye. Now look through the prism and line up the object in the distance from which you are taking the bearing. Line up the object with the prism slit and the sight line marked on the lid window. Then allow the compass card to settle. Note – at night this process will be harder, simply because you will need to find a suitable object on the horizon from which to take your bearing. Whilst on the Brecon Beacons or Scottish Highlands, there can be very few objects from which to take a bearing. This usually means that you will need to take more regular readings in order to keep on the right bearing.

Step 3

Whilst looking through the prism you will see that the sight line on the window superimposes on the graduations that are visible on the outer ring of the compass card. Whichever graduation mark lines up with the sight line on the lid window that is the bearing you require. Each graduation on the outer ring represents one degree.

USING THE COMPASS TO TAKE A BEARING FROM A MAP

Step 1

Lay your map down on a level, flat surface (this is very important).

Step 2

Use the sight line access of the compass to adjust the map so that its grid lines lie correctly north and south.

Step 3

Now draw a line on the map from your present position to your destination.

Step 4

Position the compass on the map directly on the line that you have just drawn. Keep the sighting prism end of the compass nearest to your present position. Open the lid of the compass fully so that it lies flat on the map. Now align the axis of the compass with the line that you have just drawn to your destination point.

Step 5

Now rotate the bezel until its luminous mark lines up with the luminous north pointer which is marked on the compass card.

Step 6

Close to the hinge of the compass you will see an index line which is marked on a luminous patch located under the bezel glass, which is marked in graduations. Read off the bearing on the bezel glass that is directly over the index line. This figure is your bearing and the direction in which you need to travel in order to reach your objective.

USING THE COMPASS AT NIGHT

A soldier on selection will need to be capable of using the prismatic compass at night. It is far harder to take accurate readings during night and in complete darkness. If it is a cloudless night, then you will have a far greater chance of locating objects on the horizon. If there is no natural light from which to identify landmarks, then your job will be a lot harder. It is recommended that any soldier going through selection should spent plenty of time on either the Brecon Beacons, or the Scottish Highlands (preferably both) becoming competent in the use of the prismatic compass.

The prismatic compass does however contain Tritium light sources which enable the compass to be used at night. Whilst viewing through the prism at night, the sight line on the lid window will not be visible. In this situation you will need to lay the lid window back to almost the horizontal position. This will then reveal a luminous marker located on the underside of the lid tab. This marker can now be used as a sight line.

FINAL TIPS

- Make sure you are fully competent at map reading and also in the use of the prismatic compass. Without these skills you will easily become lost and disorientated.

- Practice using a prismatic compass in all types of weather conditions if possible. If you can use the prismatic compass competently, then your time during phase 1 selection will be a lot easier.

- In particular, use the compass at night and in complete darkness. A night where there is no natural light from the stars or moon is preferable.

A FEW FINAL WORDS

We've now reached the end of the guide and have covered a tremendous amount of information that you will find useful if you are going forward for selection. You will have noticed that throughout the guide the emphasis has been on desire and a will to succeed. I place these as a greater priority than fitness levels. Yes fitness is important, but your mindset is even more so. Tune your mind to focus on the end goal and never let it detract away from it!